THE JANUARY 2015 SCOTT REPORT — 4TH QUARTER 2014 SUMMARY
BEVERLY HILLS REAL ESTATE FACTS, VALUES, TRENDS AND OPPORTUNITIES FOR HOMEOWNERS AND BUYERS

2015 Outlook + 4th Quarter 2014 Reports

Dear Friend,

Welcome to *The Scott Report, January 2015.* This report contains the most up-to-date market information, statistics as well as our current market conditions. There are practical tips for you whether you're selling a home, or buying, or know someone who is.

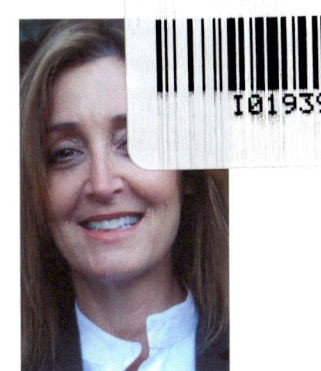

Victoria Scott, Editor
The Scott Report;
CEO *Victoria Scott Estates*
at Coldwell Banker
Beverly Hills North

This report will put you in the direct center of the January 2015 market. It gives you a birds-eye view and arms you with practical advice and recommendation to assist you in achieving your real estate aims in 2015, in Beverly Hills and the Westside.

I hope you find this edition useful and encouraging – that is its purpose.

My wish is to serve the real estate community and the needs of those who live here, and those who want to live here, in the most professional and preeminent way.

Enjoy the photos and a little of Beverly Hills nostalgia too!

It has been a pleasure and privilege to compile this quarter's Report for you. It is truly a labor of love!

Victoria Scott
Editor, The Scott Report, Beverly Hills

P.S. Please be sure to read my Open Letter to Beverly Hills Homeowners on page 53. It contains valuable information about gaining the most from your real estate agent.

The 2015 Scott Report (4th Quarter 2014)

Copyright © 2015 Victoria Scott Estates, Inc

Published by Scott Report Publishers
Victoria Scott Estates, Inc
Coldwell Banker, 301 North Canon Drive, Suite E,
Beverly Hills CA 90210

www.californiamoves.com/victoria.scott

All rights reserved. No part of this report may be reproduced or transmitted in any form without the express permission in writing from the publisher, except by a reviewer who may quote brief passages for review purposes.

ISBN-13: 978-0692375938
ISBN-10: 0692375937

Printed by CreateSpace
Available from Amazon.com and Amazon worldwide

The January 2015 Scott Report — 4th Quarter 2014 Summary
BEVERLY HILLS REAL ESTATE FACTS, VALUES, TRENDS AND OPPORTUNITIES FOR HOMEOWNERS AND BUYERS

CONTENTS

4th Quarter 2014 Summary — 2015 Emerges with Strength and Opportunity	5
Six Important Points About Selling and Moving	9
Stan Richman 2014 Overview and 2015 Forecast	13
SPECIAL SUPPLEMENT 11-Point January 2015 Self Home Valuation	19

PART 2
USEFUL (STILL CURRENT) ARTICLES FROM PAST EDITIONS

Beverly Hills Continues To Be a Unique Market	27
Proposition 60/90 — A Real Tax Benefit For Ages 55+	27
Accurately (Optimally) Pricing Your Beverly Hills Home	28
Survey of Sellers and Buyers	29
Expert Advice for Beverly Hills Sellers and Buyers	31
Sage and Timely Advice From Real Estate Veteran, Stan Richman	43
From The Desk of Victoria Scott: An Open Letter To B.H. Home Owners	53
Professional Real Estate Services Offered by Victoria Scott Estates	58

The January 2015 Scott Report — 4th Quarter 2014 Summary
BEVERLY HILLS REAL ESTATE FACTS, VALUES, TRENDS AND OPPORTUNITIES FOR HOMEOWNERS AND BUYERS

January 2015 Beverly Hills Real Estate Reports
2014 best ever Beverly Hills and Westside year—2015 off to a great start

2014 was the best year ever in high end sales. Beverly Hills and the Westside ended the year with 436 closed sales of 5 plus million, versus 396 for 2013. There were 130 closed sales of 10 plus million, versus 95 in 2013. We had 30 closed sales of 20 plus million, versus 14 for 2013. Of the 30, 15 were over 30 million, verses 5 for 2013 and 8 over 40 million, versus 2 in 2013. The largest number of the 30, twenty plus million dollar sales were in Holmby Hills with 10 sales, followed by:
- Malibu with 6 sales.
- Beverly Hills with 4 sales.
- Bel Air with 3 sales.
- Beverly Hills PO with 2 sales.
- Brentwood with 2 sales.
- Sunset Strip with 1 sale.
- Santa Monica with 1 sale, and
- Palisades with 1 sale.

The breakdown of buyers are:
- 16 American.
- 3 English.
- 2 Russian.
- 1 Saudi Arabian.
- 1 Kuwaiti.
- 1 Chinese.
- 1 Indonesian.
- 1 Persian.
- 1 Ukranian.
- 1 Swedish.
- 1 Kazakstans, and
- 1 European (I am unsure of which European country).

2015 is off to a great start. There have been 19 closed sales of 5 plus million so far this year, versus 16 at this time last year. There have been 7 closed sales of 10 plus million, versus 4 at this time last year. We have already closed two sales of over 30 million this year and there are 4 pending sales of 20 plus million at the moment. It looks like it is going to be another amazing year for the high end.

The latest data from California Association of Realtors (CAR) reports the 2014 average annual appreciation as being 4.9%. The leveling-off and stabilizing of appreciation is good news for both buyers and sellers but the market is still quite strongly tipped to favor sellers.

One of those favors is buyer confidence. Confidence is strong with a more predictable and manageable housing market and low mortgage interest rates.

With interest rates this low, buyers can diversify their investments and not have to pay cash for their family or investment home. Buying leverage still exists. Rather than buyers feeling they need to wait and wisely time their home purchase (which many felt during the 3rd and 4th quarter of 2014), greater "freedom" to buy now is being felt.

During the 3rd and 4th Quarter 2014, many buyers anticipated the market "soon topping out" and waited for a good deal. As we step into 2015, the good deals are those right before buyers' eyes. Choices are still limited by low inventory, but with interest rates currently low and stable, buyers feel confident and are still making quick, decisive purchases.

Sellers are benefiting from buyer confidence with solid, decisive purchasing.

The January 2015 Scott Report — 4th Quarter 2014 Summary
BEVERLY HILLS REAL ESTATE FACTS, VALUES, TRENDS AND OPPORTUNITIES FOR HOMEOWNERS AND BUYERS

Buyer satisfaction has gradually improved during 2014 compared to 2013 and will continue to improve as we move forward in 2015. Buyers are more satisfied with the homes they've purchased as compared the 2013 C.A.R. survey.

Beverly Hills sellers can feel confident to introduce their homes for sale with bravado. Serious, qualified buyers still have too few choices throughout the city. The market is still tipped in the seller's favor. Inventory is trickling in but still too slowly to satisfy the demand. We live in one of the most desired cities in the world where demand exists locally, nationally and internationally.

As we go to press, there are only 49 homes for sale in Beverly Hills city, and 77 in Beverly Hills Post Office – a total of 126. This number remains considerably short of meeting buyer-demand. The next 60 days will set the tone for 2015.

Bottom line for sellers: if you are ready to sell, now is a strong time.

2015 BEGINS IN SELLERS' FAVOR

A major reason the spring market has come early 2015 is the very busy 4th quarter 2014. Historically, the real estate market slows down in the 4th quarter right around Daylight Savings Time early November and throughout December. Usually, there is a surge of inventory (new homes listed for sale) after January 1st. This new inventory takes a few weeks to reach optimum market exposure and build new year momentum. But because the 4th Quarter 2014 was so busy the market has not lost its pace; there is great momentum carrying us forward into 2015. Expect optimum results from listing and marketing your home during the 1st and 2nd quarters of 2015.

Always discuss your selling or buying plans with a good agent. Start discussions early – in the preliminary stages of getting your home ready for sale, or starting the buying process. There are definite advantages in speaking with, and planning with, a professional. Nothing beats having good, professional help which, for sellers, usually leads to you garnering greater profits and, for buyers, a more satisfactory home purchase.

CASE EXAMPLE

Let's say a home comparable to yours sells just as you are ready to have yours listed for sale. Having your home announced for sale during the sale or directly after that comparable property goes into escrow allows your home to catch the slipstream created by all the marketing and exposure (web site, brochure, advertising and open houses) of the other home. All of the work, exposure and interest that house created – while setting a price benchmark – is a readymade advantage for yours. Prospective buyers have an immediate sense of value. Your property is hot!

A professional agent knows this, spots it, and advises you accordingly about when and how to list your home for sale. For instance, we daily scan and analyze the Beverly Hills market. This enables us to advantageously position seller's homes in the slipstream of other market activity and achieved sales prices in the city, and to market to buyers who have already proven their qualified interest in similar homes. A seller's home can be priced with greater precision and gain a jump on attracting prospective buyer's interest.

You may want to gain pre-sale exposure, to test the market and the level of interest your home attracts in the early stages. These are all things worth discussing with your agent.

> "A professional agent knows this, spots it, and advises you accordingly about when and how to list your home for sale."

The January 2015 Scott Report — 4th Quarter 2014 Summary
Beverly Hills Real Estate Facts, Values, Trends and Opportunities for Homeowners and Buyers

RECENT BUILDING STANDARDS UPDATE

In an effort to reduce the growing popularity of "oversized" homes where a property is "all house" with virtually no land, Beverly Hills city has mandated restrictions on the square footage a home can be in proportion to the land (lot) size.

Overall, we consider this restriction to be positive. If building continued to be oversized and disproportional to lot size, Beverly Hills would, in three or four decades, become a garden-less city. Much of its charm is its well-proportioned, green and spacious city feel. Most current residents want Beverly Hills to retain that charm. And the city is listening!

It has been going through several building regulations and restrictions transitions. West Hollywood and other cities are facing the same challenge and are now implementing size and style restrictions.

Other cities have solved this by declaring an Historical Preservation Overlay Zone (HPOZ) in certain neighborhoods and sections of neighborhoods. These regulate the maintaining of a property's exterior to the original style of the home (including landscaping).

They have assigned HPOZ committees with the power to shut down – even midway through construction – any item that steps out of the original integrity of the home and neighborhood. Anytime you see a property designated HPOZ and/or Mills Act there will be specific improvements and/or changes you can and cannot make.

HPOZ: Before you buy or sell in a designated HPOZ area, please realize your restrictions (or ask us about them). Here's a useful website:

http://preservation.lacity.org/hpoz/la
(click on the specific neighborhood link)

> "The largest value calculation dynamic for new builds is square footage. It's pretty simple in most cases: the more square feet the higher the value. For a builder it is simple arithmetic."

If you are interested in more specific information, I would recommend directing all inquiries to the President or named contact of the HPOZ committee for that neighborhood. Their contact information is listed on the website. HINT: positions on these committees are strictly voluntary, so response times are not always immediate. Patience is worthwhile. There are also HPOZ meetings listed, generally bi-monthly, and all are welcome to attend. My experience with these committees is very positive so do avail yourself of them if needed.

MILLS ACT: Homes under Mills Act contract (preserving the interior as well as exterior) do receive a sizable property tax discount during the contract period. Visit the Mills Act website for all information:

www.preservation.lacity.org/incentives/mills-act
For Beverly Hills visit: www.beverlyhills.org
– search "Mills Act Pilot Program"

INCREASE IN BUILDING ACTIVITY

There has been a surge in builders/developers coming into the marketplace – mostly for investment (buy, demolish, build and resell) – throughout the last two years and spilling into 2015.

Although there are commissioned "new builds" (buyers acquiring properties, building to their own specifications with the intention of living in the finished property – known as "end users") these are in slightly smaller proportion compared with most of the new construction.

The majority of new construction in Beverly Hills is by investors, building for immediate resale.

Also showing a slight trend are builders/investors buying property, investing in the architectural renderings and applying for the necessary permits, then selling "the vision" with all the preliminary work done. All that's left for the new owner is to break ground. Great profits are possible. One case in point is a property in Trousdale which sold in March of 2014 for $9,800,000. The new owner had all plans submitted and permits pulled, ready to break ground, and sold it inclusive of the new design for $15,000,000 six months later in December 2014 – a handsome, quick $5,200,000 profit.

The largest value calculation dynamic for new construction is square footage. It's pretty simple in most cases: the more square feet, the higher the value. For a builder it is simple arithmetic. Even though it is impossible to accurately predict market appreciation two or three years down the line, anytime there is a view property or a home with a large, build-able lot, the demand is high and the investment has been proven sound.

This is why building and developing has been (as BH property values skyrocketed throughout 2013-14) and still is on the rise throughout the city. Every site has its own unique value and price.

Note: The price per square foot of $2361 on the Trousdale sale was calculated on the existing 6,300 square foot home, not the 15,000 sq ft home that was approved for building. Lot size is 24,908.

THE NEW BUILDING REGULATIONS AT A GLANCE

As of December 4, construction and major remodels of single-family homes within central Beverly Hills fall under an updated set of development mandates. Approved amendments speak to building heights, side setbacks, and landscaping and parking requirements. Major amendments are listed here:
- Maximum height of the home will be tied to its roof type.
- Porte Cocheres must be set back a minimum of 4 feet from the front setback line.
- Houses north of Santa Monica Boulevard now have a maximum roof plate height.
- Light wells may not be located in either front or side setback areas, except if screened in street-side setbacks.
- Properties south of Santa Monica Boulevard: the 9-foot wide side setback required on one side of the house for the first 38 feet will be extended along the entire length of the property.
- Walls or fences higher than 18 inches in the front setback must be located a minimum of 3 feet from the front lot line and the surrounding area landscaped.
- There must be a 2-foot wide area of landscaping along the entire length of each required side yard (certain exceptions apply).
- Additional parking spaces are required for new homes. Additional parking may also be required for added bedrooms in existing homes.

For full information about the new ordinance visit: www.beverlyhills.org/r1standards
or telephone 310-285-1135

MORTGAGE MONEY IS CHEAP: RATES SERVE BOTH SELLERS AND BUYERS

As we go to press, mortgage rates for a 30-year fixed Jumbo loan (a first trust deed amount over $625,500) are 3.75%.

Rates are slightly less for conforming loans (a loan amount under $625,500). For a 15-year fixed rate Jumbo loan the rate is 3.375%

These low rates offer wonderful opportunities for buyers. As rates increase, the same payment for which each buyer needs to qualify, buys less house. The low rates also present richer opportunities for sellers as buyers are able to buy more house for less money (therefore offer premium prices).

If your home is on the market for many months, if the rate gradually increases by that token, your home's value can soften. Low rates and an appreciating, even a leveling market is an ideal position for sellers.

THE JANUARY 2015 SCOTT REPORT — 4TH QUARTER 2014 SUMMARY
BEVERLY HILLS REAL ESTATE FACTS, VALUES, TRENDS AND OPPORTUNITIES FOR HOMEOWNERS AND BUYERS

THIS CLIENT CONVERSATION BROUGHT OUT SIX IMPORTANT POINTS ABOUT MOVING

As I sat down to start writing the January 2015 Report, I received a call from an old friend who told me she is planning to move out of state to be near her children. Our conversation brought up a number of important points about moving (and about buyers).

In a nutshell: She and her spouse have been in their home over 25 years. It is a modest home on a large property with a large guest house. I asked her why she wants to move now.

"The upkeep is too much work for me now, and I want to stay close to my children." Both good reasons to move.

"Have you spoken to any real estate agents"?

"I spoke with two. Both I liked and felt as if I could trust them. Both had knowledge of the area, but one seemed to have one or two buyers interested in the area already. I think I might choose her."

Thus began the conversation I like to have with all clients. The "why" and "when" and "how" of moving is important to understand so that the agent can fit into and serve the client and everything involved in the client's move.

She had already researched the city she is moving to (her target is April or May), and has selected an agent there to actively look for properties for her. Her end game is in play.

She has already started de-cluttering, as she referred to it – "an enormous amount of accumulation over the last 25 years." Her three piles -- donate or sell, throw away and keep. (I know those three piles only too well!) I asked if she needed any help with it (there are specialists we put clients in touch with if they need help).

"No, my family is all pitching in."

Her home, built in 1950 and never updated, on a half an acre of attractive land, has appeal for two main types of buyers – either a private buyer who is keen to update or refurbish it throughout, or a builder/developer who would remodel or rebuild and then re-sell. And so this brings up an important question. How much work should she do before she puts up her house for sale?

I always advise making a house look as clean and clutter free as possible. Attractiveness sells. A clean, nicely painted interior and exterior sells. So even if a property is original, as my friend's is, it is worth it to at least de-clutter, clean and touch-up the paintwork, and clean and trim the landscaping.

"Curb appeal" also plays a big factor for the majority of buyers. Even a builder will feel something about the location, the site, immediately upon approaching the front door. And someone who wants to add on and update is looking for that special setting.

My friend has an electric gate and a long driveway but the gate stopped working some time ago. It rests in the open position. Repairing the gate is worthwhile.

There is something about the first impressions that last and spark imagination. In this case, potential buyers can imagine driving up to their new home at the top of a long

> **Did You Know?**
>
> The Beverly Hills Speedway, whose center was located about where South Bedford Drive and Gregory Way intersects, existed between 1920-24, was then developed by Walter G McCarty. He turned the 200 acre plot into 837 residential and commercial plots all the way and including the Beverly Wilshire Hotel. Hence, the street McCarty Drive!

The January 2015 Scott Report — 4th Quarter 2014 Summary
Beverly Hills Real Estate Facts, Values, Trends and Opportunities for Homeowners and Buyers

driveway set behind electric gates – beautiful!

Things like this are important. Buying a home is, or at least partially, emotional, so to present the home in its best light is important and effective in helping a buyer feel its beauty and decide to buy. Where romance is alive and well sales occur!

Doing some exterior as well as interior paintwork is worthwhile. A clean and fresh look and feel sells well.

There is a point where every dollar you invest in de-cluttering, cleaning and painting comes back to you at the sale – and sometimes with "profit." There is a delicate balance between which items are important, and which can be left alone. It depends on which type of buyer your home will most appeal to. I call it "buyer profiling." In other words, having a distinct feel for who will inhabit the home based on its location, layout and condition.

If your home is in excellent condition, then it is worth repairing or replacing items in readiness for a "move-in" buyer. In my friend's case, repairing and replacing or modernizing is not worth investing in because that house can appeal to a buyer who will want to do their own work. In her case cleaning, painting and minor repair is enough.

Next – because her ideal move date is April or May (three or four months away), I advised her to list her house now, rather than waiting until March, the so-called "spring selling season" as some agents may advise. There are a couple of reasons for that recommendation:

> "It takes just a little skillful negotiating by your agent to achieve this – and virtually any other creatively structured agreement that serves both parties."

1, Pricing (or should I say mis-pricing). Homeowners and agents can price using market research and their best guess – which a lot of the time is spot on.

But ultimately the market determines value. If the initial price is too high which, in this market and with her particular price range (under $3.5M) takes 21-30 days to determine if it's priced too high. Then she can reduce the price and look forward to putting together a deal "at the right price" within the next 30 days. So 60 days may have lapsed on the front end leaving her just 60 days to close and move. Listing now, in January, rather than March, allows her the time for the possible delay due to pricing or any delay having to due with the buyer's performance.

2, If her home appeals to a builder or developer, a seller can ask for a 30 day or even 60 day lease back for as little as $1. Before a builder/developer can even break ground, he or she must first acquire plans and pull permits which can take up to a year. This allows you, the seller, to close escrow on the house but not have to move immediately. All of these options are negotiable and should be a agreeable to both parties.

Knowing that you have sold your house makes it so easy to buy your next home. You know to the dollar how much you can invest and how much you can keep in reserve for decorating, modifications, improvements and landscaping. You can schedule to the week when you'd like to move. It's a near-perfect scenario!

It takes just a little negotiating skill by your agent to achieve this, and/or virtually any other creatively structured agreement that serves both parties. Virtually anything is possible, so I always ask my sellers and buyers what their ideal scenario would be and then set out to achieve those for them. I can serve those desires in the most creative and fair way for all parties.

Did You Know?

The design of the four original Beverly Hills streets – Rodeo, Beverly, Canon and Crescent Drives between Santa Monica and Sunset Blvd – were said to have been inspired by the curves of a women.

Ninety-five out of 100 times it works and satisfies everyone involved especially in a market were there are insufficient numbers of homes for sale to satisfy buyer demand.

NOTE: Whether an agent represents a buyer or seller an agent's fiduciary (financial responsibility) is to the *seller*.

Todays buyers tend to be flexible on terms because they are unsure when another home of their liking will come up for sale.

When I represent a buyer who is interested in making an offer on a house, my first activity is to find out what the seller's circumstances and desires are. These are discussed with the buyer and an offer is structured that fits snuggly in with the seller. In doing this, my buyer's offer is a good fit for the particular seller (especially during these times of multiple offers on most Beverly Hills properties). Of course, the offer has to be an equitable deal for the buyer. The key is to serve seller and buyer alike.

What about my friend? Well, if this ends up as being her scenario, she will have a single move which makes the transition smoother and less stressful. Moving to a new city always takes some adjustments beyond selling a home, then buying another home. A smart, well-planned and smooth selling and buying process, and transaction, is important whenever you sell or buy.

When you list your home for sale, your agent should have his or arms wrapped around the entire picture in order to serve you best (see "Choosing a Real Estate Agent, page 53).

HINTS and WISDOM

1, When your house is ready for sale, the first two weeks are crucial. Avoid or delay making plans at home during these first two weeks. Lightly live in your home. Leave it readily available for the first viewings. If you want fish for dinner during the first two weeks, go out to your favorite restaurant instead!

2, Expect two back-to-back, 3-hour duration open houses. Give yourself 3.5 to 4 hours out of the house for both open houses. A successful open house leads to showings – usually within days of each open house. This will be an indication of how well your home is priced. So throughout the marketing period of your home, be sure to allow your agent easy access for each private showing. Leave it (as near as possible) in the exact condition it was in for the open houses. We (and every good agent) will help you set the stage for each showing.

3, If you have a pet (my friend has four dogs), consider where you can keep them (out of the house) during each open house and each private showing. Board and care? A neighbor or relative?

4, When people visit your home, you want them to relax and take their time. You never want to rush them out. Actually, the longer they stay the more apt they are to consider making an offer. They begin to feel the joy and possibility of the home, which can happen during an un-rushed visit. Literally, you want them to feel at home.

5, Some potential and serious buyers request two or three showings or may show up early at the open house and stay awhile. They often gauge other interested parties before they make an offer. Time and freedom for prospective buyers should be granted.

Another point here. It is mostly counter-productive and not recommended for an owner to be present during open houses and private showings. Buyers can't relax, and can't speak freely. Having the owner present often intimidates buyers from asking questions. Open houses and private showings should be relaxed so that prospective buyers can freely ask questions and reveal

> "These are discussed with the buyer and an offer is structured which fits snuggly in with the you, the seller."

The January 2015 Scott Report — 4th Quarter 2014 Summary
Beverly Hills Real Estate Facts, Values, Trends and Opportunities for Homeowners and Buyers

their real interest.

Some buyers still play "poker" but that's okay! I like to make it easy for them to have or be able to ask for all of the information they want or need. I am an open book with all sellers and buyers. Transparency puts everyone at ease and trust is quickly gained (very important). The whole experience and everyone involved is the better for it – including your bottom line profit as a seller (which, after all, is the whole point!).

6, After you've come to terms and have an accepted offer, make the house available again for the buyer to do his due diligence with all inspections.

NOTE: As of November 24, 2014 the California Residential Purchase Agreement and Joint Escrow Instructions (offer) contract was revised. It now puts the onus of the Termite (wood destroying pests) report and repair on the buyer instead of the seller.

Ever since I began in real estate (1978) the termite report and the corrective repair work and/or cost has been the responsibility of the seller. Not any more! From November 24, 2014 the seller is not responsible for providing a report and the repair estimates are negotiable. It is now part of a *buyer's* due diligence. However, the new contract still maintains the results of the inspections, repairs and costs to be negotiated between buyer and seller.

Bottom line: as a seller, don't be concerned, it is now the buyer's responsibility to include termite and wood destroying pests as part of his or her investigations. Additional buyer inspections may include; chimney, sewer line, mold, geological reports. A buyer may opt to have some or none of these inspections, it is entirely up to him.

Remember a buyer's offer is made reflective of "everything they can see" or are "made aware of" about the property at the time of their offer. Additional discoveries made during the early stages of the escrow, either through seller disclosures or inspections are up for dollar amount negotiation.

If you think it is likely a builder/developer will purchase your house, you need not be concerned about any inspections other than, perhaps, the geological report because a builders intention is to remove the existing structure(s).

In my friend's case, I'd say she has a 50% probability a builder will be interested in buying her property. So she need not have any unnecessary concerns about the overall condition of the house.

> "Having an agent who knows your area well is invaluable. Their local knowledge instils confidence in buyers who are looking to buy in your area."

The reason her situation is noteworthy, is that it shows someone who is motivated to sell and is looking for the most efficient profitable way to go about it, starting from the very beginning. Her situation is very similar to most sellers right now, who are in various stages and degrees of this set of circumstances.

Discussing, planning and mapping are all parts of the selling process. A good agent will visit your home and do a market evaluation, which will give you a definitive range for your asking price. Then they help you to organize the sequence of events to bring you to successful results – selling your home for it's optimum price in your optimum time frame.

NOTE: Having an agent who knows the neighborhood well is invaluable. They have authority and instill confidence in buyers who are looking in your area, all of which has a strong positive affect on your final price!

THE JANUARY 2015 SCOTT REPORT — 4TH QUARTER 2014 SUMMARY
BEVERLY HILLS REAL ESTATE FACTS, VALUES, TRENDS AND OPPORTUNITIES FOR HOMEOWNERS AND BUYERS

STAN RICHMAN 2014 OVERVIEW AND 2015 FORECAST

Stan Richman, Manager/VP
Coldwell Banker Beverly Hills
North Office

In a nutshell - 2014 was somewhat like 2013 – a lot of speculation and building in all areas from the high 50 million to the 2 million dollar price range all across the board.

I don't think I have ever seen that many speculators all across the board. A lot of people that have never speculated are now in the market place. It's driving up prices a lot in all areas.

The lack of 1 million to 3 million dollar homes has really been hit the hardest. That's where the majority of people want to buy in all Westside areas. There is less inventory and more speculators. The demand in that price range is greater than ever before. The average sale has gone way up. In 2013 it was 1.8 million; in 2014, in our office, the average was 2.2 million. That's a pretty big jump in one year, although we had a lot of large sales, which throws off the curve a little bit.

Our number of property sales are about the same as last year – we are doing about 1600 units for the year (at Coldwell Banker). But across the board it's really quite amazing. The activity across the board is multiple offers for the 1-3 million dollar homes. I always speak about the 1 million and over because that's really where the brunt of the business is.

Beverly Hills, per square foot, has risen probably 20% in the last two years – that's kind of remarkable. Across the board. Again, a lot of speculation, a lot of people want to build – about 10-20% that want to build. That's a lot actually, because the building process is 2-3 years. But there are those people who want big lots – especially the 20,000 sq ft and over

> "There are people who want big lots, especially 20,000 sq ft and more in the Flats. There is still real demand for those."

lots in the flats. There is still a real demand for that. A done home in BH anywhere from $8-12 million would be gone in a second if we could get more homes like those that are move-in and done.

There are a couple of builders trying to get all of the permits pulled and the plans approved and then selling that package versus actually following through on the build. We haven't seen enough of it to call it a real trend. They can get the plans and permits but it has to be a specific style for a specific client so it's pretty hard to fit someone directly into what they designed to build. Except for some of the contemporaries in the Hills, they seem to work a little bit better. As for the flats, I haven't seen it done yet.

Out of the 10-20%, I don't know how many are private commissions versus build and sale/re-sale. We will know more of what is happening this year as there will be some projects that finish up this year. I don't know who is actually going to build and who is going to sell it off. I would say is 10% for resale purposes and 10% for a specific client, that's off the top of my head. I'm talking about Beverly Hills, some areas there is a little bit more spec – Doheny Estates and the Bird streets a little bit more spec.

One wonderful thing about last year is that our buyer pool for us is so diversified. Most of the clients are local or from New York or the East Coast. About 70 percent of buyers are still American, I'd say. We do have about 30% who are coming from all over the world, and they are paying cash. The majority are still local people that have either inherited money, made money, or have generational money. We are

The January 2015 Scott Report — 4th Quarter 2014 Summary
Beverly Hills Real Estate Facts, Values, Trends and Opportunities for Homeowners and Buyers

seeing a lot of that, more now than ever before.

But 30 percent are coming onto Beverly Hills for the first time, so that's going to be interesting as far as future dynamics.

One other thing that stands out from 2014 is bigger dollar numbers. We have had a 70 million dollar sale in Trousdale. That kind of aberration is unbelievable – not the consistent market. Someone who just sold a company or inherited giant wealth is going to do that, especially in Beverly Hills. So it's those unique things, that everybody reads about, which does a lot for our market internationally. We are still cheaper than London and New York, by far.

New York still has a bigger demand base, they have more of an international base than we do. New York real estate has always – for the last 5-10 years – been strong. It has a little to do with New York's proximity to Europe, not just Europe though. Russia too. It's pretty diversified. People with money have always come to New York and now some of that money is coming here. We've never had as high of a percentage before.

I think the reason is the change in LA. It's more cosmopolitan than it ever has been. The wealthy want to be here. The weather of course is the number one factor. And now that there is some real substantial housing that they can go into, they are drawn here. We've never had those big homes before. People would go to Bel Air and get some land but they would get 12,000 square feet. Now there are 18–25,000 square foot homes here. It's a big thing to be able to have properties with that size of living in Beverly Hills. We will see where this is all going, it's all so new to Westside real estate.

> "One thing that stands out is bigger dollar numbers. We have had a $70 million sale in Trousdale. That is unbelieveable!"

The trend is quite revealing. The trend is definitely going up and up. Specifically, last year we sold a 74 million dollar house with 4 acres in Holmby Hills to a guy from China. That was unbelievable. We had another guy from Sweden. Just look at the diversification, we have never had that before.

I think the only negative about the last few years is the community's mansionization. It is affecting a lot of areas.

New regulations are putting a stop to much of that but even areas that weren't so involved are getting involved, for instance, Cheviot Hills. There are going to be regulations now in every community, I think. If you look, on every other street there is construction going on. The building regulations are going to change land value a little bit because of limiting what can be build, so we will see to what degree it does.

Luckily most of our city is single family housing whereas in New York and London it's projects. We still don't have that. Beverly Hills will hopefully get a big project in the next couple of years and maybe some downtown. Santa Monica has one now. We need more of that, we don't have enough. We don't have enough density of projects like that, that are nicely done.

It changes areas. Right now, I'd say, Venice, per square foot, probably is as expensive as any place. Now with Google and other companies locating in Playa Vista, you will see a change in the next 5 years that will be phenomenal. It's going to transition to giant numbers which we have never seen there before. Santa Monica already has transitioned to big property values. Next people will go to Venice and those areas

Did You Know?

The original lot prices for the 500 blocks of Canon Crescent, Beverly and Rodeo Drives started at $900 in 1906. Today that same $900 equals $23,684. The earth of those lots alone are worth 4,000,000.

The January 2015 Scott Report — 4th Quarter 2014 Summary
Beverly Hills Real Estate Facts, Values, Trends and Opportunities for Homeowners and Buyers

which are already becoming cost prohibitive as it is. There are going to be some changes in areas that they have never seen, which is exciting because it gives us more diversification. You'll have young, wealthy people or young people with good salaries working down there and now want to live nearby.

So we'll see… Playa Vista is going to be built out. Just go down Jefferson Blvd – that whole street took ten years but it's going to be done.

So on the whole 2014 was not much of a change from 2013 except for some of the bigger sales – although we had some big sales in 2013 as well. It's going to be that same kind of mix this year too – as long as we don't have an earthquake, god forbid. A major earthquake changes the dynamics very quickly. The 94' earthquake really stopped everyone for a couple of years. We had people leaving the city, and property values reflected that.

That aside, 2015 will be as busy as the past two years, especially with interest rates as low as they are at the moment. It always hurts when prices are rising because the person who wants to sell says "where am I going to go"? If the price has risen that high, even though they have equity they are saying "Do I really want to step to the next level and go from a 2 to a 4 million dollar house"? Or they may want to leave, and have to find a place to go before they sell. We get a lot of that.

Appreciation has slowed to (currently) 4.9% rather than 20% per annum, so it is much settled. In some areas it's more than 4.9%. Every area is a little different. It depends on specific streets, flat land, views versus non-views. You can go to any of the Bird streets on the Sunset Strip and if you've got a great view you can realize sometimes 25% more. You have the same lot, maybe, as across the street, but the view has added 25% or more. So appreciation is all relative.

> " Every area is a little different. It depends on specific streets, flat land, views versus non-views…. you can sometimes realize 25 percent more. "

The flats are probably leveling right now, the prices went way up over the last two years. Although there's a lot of demand for completely done homes, there might be strong appreciation on a home in the flats that's done or brand new – we don't have enough right now that fills that demand. We have a couple of older Spanish, nicely redone homes but I don't know if that's the taste of today's buyer. So it's going to be interesting to see where all of this goes in the next 6 months.

Builders and speculators feel somewhat optimistic about 2015 but the prices have gone up so that scares them a little bit. That's why I think you will see more people try to sell land with plans or try and sell a package and make their profit. It won't be as much profit but it will save them spending the two years to build it. That's going to be an interesting part of 2015 to see who does it that way, to see if it's a trend or not. We have a lot of new people that are speculating so we'll see.

My advice to home owners who are considering selling but haven't really stuck a pin in the calendar yet, is that these upward cycles don't go on forever. Also money has never been this cheap. So, you've got two factors – it's like picking a stock at the top. If you are going to do it like that you risk a fall. We don't know when the next fall will be but there *will* be a fall, there is no question about that. I've seen three cycles since I have been here so you know it will change. Anybody that has any urgency or non-urgency, always – with respect to having a place to move – would be crazy not to take what they can now and run! I mean, if there ever was "good timing" that you could see ahead of time, I would say now is that good timing!

There is no question that I would encourage someone to sell now rather that waiting to sell sometime later this year. There is no question. I am a big believer

The January 2015 Scott Report — 4th Quarter 2014 Summary
BEVERLY HILLS REAL ESTATE FACTS, VALUES, TRENDS AND OPPORTUNITIES FOR HOMEOWNERS AND BUYERS

in the "bird in the hand." That is if you have a place to go or you are leaving the city especially. Or you are changing into a small condo, or you're retiring. Take the money and feel good about it.

It is a sellers' market still, and it will continue to be this year but who knows next year? You know, we have had four very strong years now, that's a pretty long cycle. I think if someone has the wherewithal to sell their home now, it's a good idea. Whether it's going into something smaller, a condo, or Palm Springs or Arizona where you can get so much more for your money.

> "It is a seller's market. If a home owner has the wherewithal to sell their home now, it is a good idea."

I believe it is impractical to sell your home privately because we never know who has a buyer from Timbuktu. Some little agent that has never sold anything comes with a buyer who would otherwise never have heard about the house. The 70 million dollar deal originally came by an agent from Studio City who had never sold anything in her career. She ended up hooking up with a local Beverly Hills agent to help her but it was her client, a client from Sweden. All due to the property's exposure. That buyer may well never have been found – may never have known about the house – had the house not been marketed and available openly.

And here's a word about pricing a home. Let's say a homeowner asks us to value their home. We value it at, let's say, between 10-13 million. The homeowner thinks it's worth 15 million yet all the comparisons show that it is worth between 10-13 million. But, especially in Beverly Hills, *you never know.* We will list it at 15 million and do our best. We will address the response from the market every 30 days and see if the seller wants to reduce the price. They might say "I don't care, I want 15 million, "take it or leave it."

Sometimes a seller will change their mind and ask us to reduce the price if the high price is not responding. As long as the seller doesn't want us to spend a lot of money continually promoting it, to the point where we are out of pocket a great deal. We still do the regular things to market the house; we still give it

The January 2015 Scott Report — 4th Quarter 2014 Summary
Beverly Hills Real Estate Facts, Values, Trends and Opportunities for Homeowners and Buyers

everything we have. The key to understand is that if it has key features like land and view or something like that then we don't know 100% for sure what price the market will bear. Maybe it could fetch one or two million more than even good comps suggest.

When you get up in the over 35 million range, there are fewer comps and therefore there might be a bigger gap in pricing. If a particular buyer really wants a particular home they're sometimes willing to pay the price. Our job is to bring as many real, prospective buyers through the house and see what happens. Anything is a possibility and we are ready to accept it for each client.

Someone asked me, the other day, if Coldwell Banker is the absolute wisest choice for a seller to come to? I believe the answer is, definitely. I believe it strongly because of our name recognition which you'll never have to sell to any potential buyer, and because of our strength in the market place.

Take a look at the year-end data. In every area on the Westside, any property over a million dollars, we

> "If a particular buyer really wants a particular home, he or she may be willing to pay the (higher) price."

own the market. So you can go to a consumer and say take a look at these sale numbers, this is who we are. We are the not the cheapest guy in town, we're not going to throw our commissions down the drain but between our BH North office and the BH South office every seller gets over 400 local agents immediately that get to see their property. All the key agents know about your home for sale quickly, across the board. The whole Westside has 2600 Coldwell Banker agents – no other company has that amount of exposure. All of the other companies have, at most, 150 agents. There is no question that this company is the wisest choice for any seller.

The January 2015 Scott Report — 4th Quarter 2014 Summary
BEVERLY HILLS REAL ESTATE FACTS, VALUES, TRENDS AND OPPORTUNITIES FOR HOMEOWNERS AND BUYERS

SPECIAL SUPPLEMENT
"Getting a Quick Idea of Your Home's Value In Today's Market"

Use Victoria Scott's Beverly Hills valuation expertise with this area-specific, 11-point check list to get a quick idea of the value of your home in this January 2015 market.

Although there is no substitute for a professional home valuation, you can get a useful approximate idea of your home's value in today's fast-moving real estate market.

Accurately valuing your home is one of the most important factors in not only preparing your house for sale but also in attracting high quality, qualified prospective buyers and achieving an expedient purchase.

11 MAIN FACTORS TO VALUATION

There are 11 main factors that go into pinpointing the value of a home. In all my years as a real estate agent, these 11 factors enable me to price client's homes with remarkably reliable results.

Before every valuation, research is conducted on recent "like" sales in the neighborhood. This speaks to current price per square foot and land values.

Every property in Beverly Hills is saleable. I mean that literally. Every home sells.

An accurately priced home sells quickly in today's market. The first offers received – in the first one to three weeks or so of market exposure – are usually the best.

OPTIMAL PRICING AND OFF-MARKET SELLING

To exorbitantly overprice (which only very occasionally a seller wants the agent to do, with a "let's try to get a jackpot" approach), even if the seller is prepared to wait many months or even a year or two for a potential buyer, usually hurts the property's true value and appeal. It weakens the market strength and position of the house. An accurate, *optimal valuation which recognizes the property's unique highest value* is the key.

Every sale has a "temperature" which is related to timing. The higher the heat, the greater the result, all around – both selling and buying. Again, accurate valuation enables the temperature to remain high with optimal interest from buyers.

Off-market sales (the industry calls them "pocket listings") do not weigh in as heavily in the comparisons. Because of their limited market exposure they usually sacrifice up to 10% of their ultimate value. Another reason you may not want to "pocket-list" your property!

The January 2015 Scott Report — 4th Quarter 2014 Summary
Beverly Hills Real Estate Facts, Values, Trends and Opportunities for Homeowners and Buyers

THE 11 FACTORS

FACTOR 1: Square footage – includes permitted and non-permitted additions and guest houses.

FACTOR 2: Lot/land size.

FACTOR 3: Location.

FACTOR 4: Amenities – i.e. pool, views, home theatre, home office, guest house, tennis court.

FACTOR 5: Condition / Year built.

FACTOR 6: Privacy – including noise.

FACTOR 7: Setting.

FACTOR 8: Light.

FACTOR 9: Emotion

FACTOR 10: History – including celebrity if any, and notorious if any.

FACTOR 11: Quality – including signature Architect, Designer.

Before we walk through each of the steps to get an approximate idea of your home's value, here are the average per square foot prices for 6 different areas, including the number of homes sold in each Beverly Hills area from July through December, 2014:

Home Prices per Square Foot
(October through December, 2014)

90210 – BH City Flats between Santa Monica Blvd and Sunset:
$1,203 per sq ft (10 homes sold)

90210 – BH north of Sunset including Trousdale:
$2,027 per sq ft (8 homes sold)★

90210 – BHPO – excluding Beverly Park:
$775 per sq ft (42 homes sold)

90210 – BHPO – Beverly Park:
1 house sold for $39,900 (5 acres of land)

90212 – South BH West of Doheny:
$863 per sq ft (9 homes sold)

90211 – East BH:
$1010 per sq ft (8 homes sold)

These figures are drawn from homes marketed through the Multiple Listing Service (MLS), therefore represent the highest per square foot averages (homes sold "off market" – which are not listed with the MLS – statistically receive lower per square foot averages).

NOTE: If you are uncertain about your home's square footage, feel free to call 310-849-8880. It takes just a few minutes to find the information for you and we can usually give it to you while you're on the phone. Alternatively, we can recommend an excellent company who can do a formal measurement report for you.

Walking Through The 11 Factors

Factor 1: Square footage is explained above.

Factor 2: Lot size and land shape provide privacy and build-ability, and have understandable impact on value. Flat or rolling land tends to command higher values than hillside. Also if your lot size is larger than average for your neighborhood, your property commands a higher than average value. The larger parcels and those with flat, park-like grounds are always in higher demand, therefore have greater value.

Factor 3: Location, including curb appeal. When your house is in Beverly Hills you already satisfy "location, location, location" with a #1 score in desirability, so in Beverly Hills, location is more about position on the street than general position.

In this market, all property, no matter where it is located in Beverly Hills, is realizing peak values.

Degrees of curb appeal impact value. If your home is on the corner of an intersection, or the driveway is difficult to get into or out of — if your street is busy, or if the gully entering your driveway is particularly deep and could hinder some cars from easy exit and access — these aspects affect value.

If a home is on a mixed zoning street, for instance with apartment houses or/and commercial property next to a house) value is affected. We don't have much mixed zoning in Beverly Hills, although in parts of south east Beverly Hills a property can be next to or back up to commercial or income properties (typically apartment buildings or duplexes) and this somewhat reduces value compared with non mixed zoning property. But again, all Beverly Hills property is currently realizing peak value.

Factor 4: Amenities. The "ultimate" in Beverly Hills lifestyle is all about hi-tech, designer kitchens, media, multi-car garages, a swimmer's pool, sometimes a separate guest house, and views (see the Stan Richman section in this edition regarding Beverly Hills lifestyle).

All of these "ultimate" aspects add value for the buyer who wants the ultimate and is ready and willing to pay for it. Usually a home will have several of these features and lack in others. Always, there is a balance between the various aspects of a home that either add or reduce value. Also if your home has "room for" any of these current lifestyle preferences, that's the next best thing and definitely pushes up the value.

Factor 5: Condition. This refers to not only how well the property is maintained but also how useable each area of the home is, age of the appliances and of heating and air-conditioning units, and roof, and the condition of the hidden features such as plumbing, electrical wiring, sewer line (the line that connects your home to the city's sewer system or septic tank, which is part of your property.

Anything that has been upgraded within 5 years brings additional value. Remember to keep all of your paid receipts until you sell your home.

Factor 6: Privacy, which includes the "noise versus peace level" of the property, affects its value.

Is your backyard private from neighbors? How peaceful versus noisy (for instance road noise) is it? Can you sit in your backyard and hear traffic noise? None of these "plusses or minuses" are "good versus bad" — they are all merely degrees of value.

Beverly Hills — because it is one of the most desirable cities in the world — is witnessed substantial population and visitor increases. Beverly Hills, in particular, is a destination city. The amount of tour buses and traffic (and population!) makes Beverly Hills more densely traveled today, which has made our city noisier over the last 15 years. The majority of homes are affected by a degree of greater busyness and noise. This is expected and therefore does not affect (reduce) value as much as it did 20 or more years ago.

However, homes that do have more privacy, peace and quiet, command a greater value for buyers who definitely want to — and can in some areas of Beverly Hills — find solace from the razzmatazz of city living.

Factor 7: Setting — ahh, one of my personal favorites! This is about how your house sits on its land. Is the house well situated on the land? Is there an indoor/outdoor feel to the house? Does your house invite you to its outdoors? Does it wrap around the pool area? Does each room have a view? Does each window have privacy? Every "yes" to these factors represents increased value.

Factor 8: Light. In today's Beverly Hills market, light equals value. The more light your home has the more appeal it has.

The January 2015 Scott Report — 4th Quarter 2014 Summary
BEVERLY HILLS REAL ESTATE FACTS, VALUES, TRENDS AND OPPORTUNITIES FOR HOMEOWNERS AND BUYERS

Home styles certainly change over the years (for instance, we are seeing an increased number of top end buyers wanting contemporary homes these days) but one aspect increases the value of nearly every property, and that is that virtually everyone loves good light.

Factor 9: Emotion. Is there something particularly wonderful or even breathtaking about your home – something that few other homes have, like an incredibly lush and landscaped backyard, a yard you never want to leave because it makes you feel so relaxed and "away from it all"? Or such an authentic design or restoration of a particular style of home – like a classic car lovingly restored? Or a breathtaking view?

These factors make you feel privileged – make you marvel. Uniqueness is its own value. If something feels as if it's one-of-a-kind, it has a great emotional appeal. These homes virtually sell themselves!

Factor 10: History. Does your home have an interesting history or some kind of celebrity lineage? The perception is if "so-and-so" lived here, or on the same street, they thought of the home and/or the street as being special, therefore others will find it special too.

If I told you that a home was responsible for raising two children that both graduated from Harvard with honors, and both were nominated for the Pulitzer Prize, the home would have positive intrigue, which translates into value.

Has the home been featured in a newspaper or magazine, won any awards, had a famous TV show or movie filmed there or on the street? One major example is the Beverly House Compound on North Beverly Drive where episode 1 of The Colbys, plus The Godfather, The Bodyguard and many other movies and TV shows were filmed.

Any such famous activity is worth noting because it creates higher interest, which usually means higher

The January 2015 Scott Report — 4th Quarter 2014 Summary
BEVERLY HILLS REAL ESTATE FACTS, VALUES, TRENDS AND OPPORTUNITIES FOR HOMEOWNERS AND BUYERS

value.

Factor 11: Quality. There is nothing like quality to add value to a home. High quality flooring, imported tiles, molding, paint work, landscaping, stonework, fountain, pool area and ironwork. This also includes architectural or designer signatures. Quality is hard to miss by anyone. We all know it, quality "feels" solid, satisfying, privileged. Quality adds substance to a house, and quality equals greater value.

A higher percentage of people want a house to already possess the attributes of quality rather than have to add them, even if they can afford them.

Finally, there are seen and unseen elements that play a part in accurately valuing a home, something you may not have considered that makes your home particularly appealing in one or more ways.

So many homes have an "invisible" yet undeniable and tangible value in the eyes of the marketplace and in attracting the right, most qualified and most quickly found buyer.

Accurate pricing of a house for sale is critical. This guide gives you a way of gaining an approximate idea of your home's value but please realize that nothing beats or can replace a professional valuation. Certainly a home should never be put on the market before having a professional valuation (see opposite for a complimentary valuation).

The more accurate the price of your house for sale is, the more smoothly and quickly a transaction usually goes.

Owning property in Beverly Hills is an honor and an achievement that many would like to lay claim. If, or when, you are ready to sell your BH home, what is certain is that you will – and for a good price too!

11-POINT CHECKLIST

Use this checklist to determine what you feel is "above average" about your house. Refer to the explanation above for each of the 11 determining factors. NOTE: if you are able to check 5 or more, your home may be worth above average price per square foot in your area.

☐ Factor 1: Sq footage (check neighborhood average above).

☐ Factor 2: Lot size (check average).

☐ Factor 3: Location, street position.

☐ Factor 4: Amenities (extras).

☐ Factor 5: Overall condition.

☐ Factor 6: Privacy / peace.

☐ Factor 7: Setting.

☐ Factor 8: Light.

☐ Factor 9: Emotional quota.

☐ Factor 10: History.

☐ Factor 11: Quality.

* The average price per square foot has jumped in this area in the 4th Quarter because of the record-breaking sale of 1181 Hillcrest Road, Beverly Hills 90210 for $70 million.

The sale of 1163 Hillcrest sold for $35 million on January 5th, 2015 will positively affect the 1st Quarter 2015 90210 North of Sunset statistics as well.

PART 2

USEFUL (STILL CURRENT)
ARTICLES FROM PAST EDITIONS

The January 2015 Scott Report — 4th Quarter 2014 Summary
Beverly Hills Real Estate Facts, Values, Trends and Opportunities for Homeowners and Buyers

BEVERLY HILLS CONTINUES TO BE A UNIQUE MARKET

The Beverly Hills real estate market is showing signs of settling down, although still appreciating. The California Association of Realtors (C.A.R.) shows that the statewide average 20% annual appreciation witnessed during these first two quarter's (and most of 2013) has slowed to about 10% this quarter (NOTE: appreciation has slowed to 4.9 percent January 2015).

C.A.R. predicts 2015 annual appreciation to drop to around 4%.

However, *Beverly Hills continues to be a unique market*. The city maintains its own value and appreciation rate, sitting at the high end of the average statewide market values and appreciation.

Nevertheless, Beverly Hills property appreciation is slowing down. Last year we saw 23% realized annual appreciation. Currently, mainly because of the higher number of homes now coming onto the market for sale, appreciation has slowed to 10% – a drop from nearly 2% per-month to under 1% per-month. Still significant but less frenzied.

Example: according to C.A.R., a property worth $2.5M one year ago has appreciated on average by 20% over the past 12 months, adding $500K to its value.

Although the above appreciation percentages are statewide statistics, the luxury Los Angeles neighborhoods – B.H. being one of the five top luxury L.A. zip codes – are always at the top end of this spectrum.

PROPOSITION 60/90 — A REAL TAX BENEFIT FOR AGES 55+

Ages 55+ can now maintain their Proposition 13 low tax base. Proposition 60/90 allows 55+ residents who sell their homes and buy or construct a new home in a qualifying county, to maintain their existing, low property tax rates.

It can be used one time only. If you sell your Beverly Hills home and purchase or construct another property of like or lesser value (appraised value) to be your primary residence, purchased within 2 years of the sale of your current home, the benefit can applied for through the county's tax assessor office and instated as long as your new purchase is in one of these qualifying California counties: Los Angeles, Alameda, Orange, Ventura, San Mateo, San Diego, Santa Clara, El Dorado, Riverside.

Prop 60/90 County Links and Telephone Nos

Los Angeles: www.assessor.lacounty.gov
(213) 974 3211

Alameda: www.acgov.org
(510) 272-3787

Orange County: www.ocgov.com/assessor
(714) 834-2746

San Mateo: www.smcare.org
(650) 363-4500

Ventura: http://assessor.countyofventura.org
(805) 654-2181

San Diego: www.sdarcc.com
(619) 531-5481

Santa Clara: www.sccassessor.org
(408) 299-2401

El Dorado: www.edcgov.us
(530) 621-5755

Riverside: www.riversideacr.com
(951) 955-6200

THE JANUARY 2015 SCOTT REPORT — 4TH QUARTER 2014 SUMMARY
BEVERLY HILLS REAL ESTATE FACTS, VALUES, TRENDS AND OPPORTUNITIES FOR HOMEOWNERS AND BUYERS

ACCURATELY (OPTIMALLY) PRICING YOUR B.H. HOME

When your property is priced well – not low, not over-high, but spot on (see "Optimal Pricing," page 19 of this edition) – prospective buyers approach the price negotiation and the buying of the house with a "premium property" mind set, rather than a discount mentality.

A premium property mind set immediately recognizes the value of a property because of its true sale price and treats the whole process with respect.

Unfortunately, for some, the "game plan" has been to over-price their property with the intention of "being haggled down" to the right market price (a negotiating style of a bygone era, an era before the Internet, where information wasn't so readily had). In this market, such a tactic often backfires on the seller.

Granted, when market prices surged so quickly during 2013 and early 2104, pricing was more of a challenge. Now that the market is beginning to level (and has levelled by January 2015) it is easier to determine a home's accurate price range.

Only a buyer with a discount mentality attempts to haggle price; to have "something for nothing" – to win extras, things "thrown in" to make the deal. Why attract this type of buyer by overpricing a home?

If your property for sale is priced too high, either intentionally or unintentionally, your agent would have to "have the talk" with you at around the 30-day mark or sooner, about price reduction. Reducing the price one, two or even three times as an attempt to catch the pulse of the market is a strategically inefficient way to sell your home. It also, in most cases, costs you more.

Properties that sit on the market too long, then are reduced in price once, sometimes twice or three times, send a definite signal to buyers that the seller is "desperate" to sell and can be negotiated down (the discount mentality) even if the seller isn't at all desperate.

Buyers' perception is that it is a distressed sale. That same mentality sets the tone for the entire escrow through to the inspection process. As things are uncovered, the buyer looks to the seller to pay or make repairs, rather then an equitable share.

My advice: if you are selling, choose to attract buyers who have a premium mentality by having your home accurately priced. Premium mentality buyers appreciate the "gift" or opportunity of buying your home at the right price. Generally, the right buyer at the right price will come along, and the escrow will tend to be much smoother overall. The transaction is equitable for both parties.

THE JANUARY 2015 SCOTT REPORT — 4TH QUARTER 2014 SUMMARY
BEVERLY HILLS REAL ESTATE FACTS, VALUES, TRENDS AND OPPORTUNITIES FOR HOMEOWNERS AND BUYERS

SURVEY OF SELLERS AND BUYERS

- Sellers report that they want most help with: negotiating, all aspects of the buying and selling process, inspections and contracts.
- The largest percentage of international buyers in the last 12 months are from China, Canada, Mexico.
- 86% of those who bought homes in Southern California are individuals as opposed to Companys LLS.
- 81% are college educated.
- 70% are married.
- Median income is 200k.
- Average age: 46 years.
- 60% are male.
- 51% were first US purchases.
- 30% own two or more additional properties.
- 20% own 6 or more additional properties
- 85% of foreign buyers only considered USA.
- 32% bought as primary residence.
- 31% bought as vacation/second home.
- 72% purchased a 4 or 5 bedroom home.
- 42% most wanted a designer kitchen.
- 26% most wanted a wine cellar.
- 9% most wanted a sauna.
- 3% most wanted a pool.
- 71% found their property on the MLS.
- 30% bought within the first two weeks of looking at homes.
- 31% bought within 3-7 weeks of looking at homes.
- 57% of the houses they bought were on the market for under 30 days.
- International buyers spend on average 5 weeks looking for property.
- Traditional buyers spend on average 10 weeks looking for property.
- 69% of international buyers paid all cash whereas only 27% of traditional buyers paid all cash.
- 65% paid either the down payment or all cash from savings accounts.
- Only 8% had difficulty bringing funds from outside the US.
- There were fewer first-time buyers in the last 12 months. This impacts the market by keeping second time buyers (the 1m+ buyer) from being able to sell their current homes in order to move up, which accordingly slows down the buyers who want to purchase a larger bigger home.
- Nearly half of buyers (46%) felt as if they "settled" on a purchase rather than chose the property they really love because of the lack of inventory and the pressure (in a seller's market) to have to decide quickly. This is a sad survey result.
- Most buyers are optimistic about the market in the next five years.
- Sellers and buyers were *satisfied* with their agent because the agent: worked hard for them (63%), negotiated a good deal (38%), helped find the best home (37%), always responded quickly (26%), and listened to their needs (13%).
- Sellers and buyers were dissatisfied with their agent because the agent: they were slow to respond (71%), didn't communicate the way the client wanted and needed (51%), communicated ineffectively (51%), was not aggressive in negotiation (40%), needed to do a better job with paperwork (13%).

The January 2015 Scott Report — 4th Quarter 2014 Summary
BEVERLY HILLS REAL ESTATE FACTS, VALUES, TRENDS AND OPPORTUNITIES FOR HOMEOWNERS AND BUYERS

EXPERT ADVICE FOR BEVERLY HILLS SELLERS AND BUYERS

If You Are Selling

The personality of your home – your home falls into one of two main categories

The first of the two categories is an older house that is now ready for improvement or redevelopment. If your home falls into this category, there is no need to ready it for sale. Renovators and developers are looking purely for lot location, size and opportunity. Beverly Hills lots alone are worth their size in gold with plenty of opportunity to sell to the right developer.

These types of properties are in very high demand today. Builders will often get into a bidding war to acquire them. They are developing this type of property for their current commissioned clients as well as for spec.

If your property is a tear down or fixer (flippable) it has a ceiling to its value to a developer. It's value is determined more as price per square foot, calculated by builders/developers both now and at the finished end. It has to pencil on the buying side, improving side, and the reselling side. All three aspects are mathematically formulated. It is more mathematical than anything else.

Today the market works in your favor as a seller. Plus interest rates are still low and the prime inventory of houses for sale is still low. This goes to make a win-win for both seller and buyer.

The good news for you if you're selling a fixer or land-value property, is that this type of purchase for a buyer is an unemotional one. For them, what you see is what you get. The bad news is there is a definite ceiling to the property's actual value, even though you may be presented with multiple offers, and a possible bidding war.

You will see exactly what your property's cash value is by the offers that come in, and there will still be at least several offers in today's market. I've seen as many as 13 of which 10 were all cash!

The exception to a property's cash-value ceiling is a buyer who is developing the property for himself. He will pay more than the land value to secure the property because he intends to live there for the forseeable. He will be the one who will pay the extra to insure your property is won by him.

The only factor which may seem to be a downside for you, is the emotional one. When you drive down your street in years to come and the property that used to be your home will no longer be there. It is sometimes sad and yet... progress and tasty redevelopment is a wonderful thing.

The amount of dollars (cash) going into complete redevelopment of these properties is uncanny. The neighborhoods we grew up in will be unrecognizable in spots in the next 5 years. But progress cannot be stopped and with this amount of wealth being poured into many of the BH neighborhoods, progress is inevitable (and on the whole good, I think).

If your home falls into this category, or perhaps you're not sure, then the question is, how much work does it need?

One way to determine it is, if it isn't cost effective for a new owner to remodel, or your home has been remodeled more than once within the last 15 years (there are only so many remodels a house can practically withstand until it makes more sense to start over) then your very livable home may be a developer's dream.

The January 2015 Scott Report — 4th Quarter 2014 Summary
Beverly Hills Real Estate Facts, Values, Trends and Opportunities for Homeowners and Buyers

Some homes have had multiple additions which can make floor plans a little irregular. These homes may also be considered as redevelopment opportunity in today's marketplace.

If your home is older and has great "bones" or floor plan, it may be a perfect candidate for a second story or remodel. This is worth more than strictly land-value.

If you're unsure, a qualified agent can help you determine how best to value and market your home, and to whom it will have greatest appeal, therefore value.

Also, if you are selling, be prepared for the possibility of receiving multiple offers. If there aren't many, don't be too concerned, it doesn't necessarily mean your home hasn't received its highest and best price. After all you only need one good buyer. Even in this seller's market, there still are buyers/investors/developers who try their luck with low-ball offers, which do not really count as serious offers.

If you receive multiple offers, your agent will lay them all out on a table, with a "cheat sheet" ledger that goes over six main points of each offer for easy comparison:

1. Price.
2. Identity of the buyer (individual, LLC, trust or company).
3. Cash or loan (if loan, down-payment amount).
4. Inspection times (how long the buyer has for his due diligence, and his financial response to his findings).
5. Escrow length.
6. Requested escrow company/title company.

These are major factors in choosing your buyer. If there's a known name, a name that brings with it integrity *and* ability, by all means make the secure choice, even if it may not be the absolute highest offer. The best deal is made up of a composite of factors – each factor representing value.

After you review all of the offers, prepare to write the counter offer(s). You and your agent may make a counter offer to every one of the offers, or maybe just to the top 2 or 3, or just chose 1 to counter to, fine tuning a point or two. Or you may even accept just the one which is outstanding on all counts.

After a deal is made and signed by both parties, indicating you've come to an acceptable agreement of all terms, your day-count starts the next business day. The escrow has officially opened – congratulations!

I would recommend designating a 2nd place deal as a "back-up offer." The purpose of designating a back-up offer is in the event the first deal does not make it through and close escrow, the second deal can be at the ready so as not to lose any of the momentum of your home's exposure, excitement, and sale.

A property that has been in and out of escrow a few times may look to other buyers as if there is possibly something wrong with it (which may translate into a lower bottom line profit for you), even if it has been the buyer who backed away and not an issue with your property. Unfortunately, in human nature, no one wants what no one wants.

This is also why one of the factors in choosing the best deal includes the agent on the other end who will help keep the transaction together until close.

> "If your home falls into this category, or you're not sure, then the question is, how much work does it need to be attractive to buyers? It can be less than you think."

The January 2015 Scott Report — 4th Quarter 2014 Summary
Beverly Hills Real Estate Facts, Values, Trends and Opportunities for Homeowners and Buyers

The second category of home in today's market is done, beautiful, and ready to sell and move into as-is. It is designed and furnished in a way everyone who is house hunting sees in the luxury house market.

If your home is done to the nines, it will be an even greater standout with greater appeal. If the square footage or lot size is ample, these homes are the ones commanding the big dollars, and sometimes will break records for prices per square foot in its neighborhood. Records are being set and broken these last six months.

The very high-end homes that reflect such an affluent quality of lifestyle really stand out. They sell quickly because their value is so blatant. These homes exceed the buyer's expectation and standout as true quality, something genuinely special.

Home staging is setting the bar. Buyers expect it today. Brokers and buyers have a certain expectation about how a home should look, mainly because of the popularity of home staging which is now a big business (it has increased 100-fold in the last 20 years in high-end real estate).

But home staging can only do so much. The decor of home staging is contemporary and clean but not necessarily the highest quality of luxury.

If your home isn't done, done, done, home staging can heal specific areas or even the entire property, both interior as well as outdoor areas.

If there's an unconventional or empty room or area in your home, staging can make sense of it. Staging explains the space and the home's lifestyle.

The success and popularity of staging is because it effectively shows the potential buyer how the home can be lived in, while making each room/space look very inviting.

> "It is worth having your own pre-sale inspections done. The more prepared you are, the faster and easier is your escrow."

Giving the home a "clean, pristine" look and feeling is an absolute plus in presenting it to buyers. A staged home sells on average 75% faster than an empty home.

The more usable living "spaces" a home has, both indoor and outdoor, the more a potential buyer is able to see himself or herself living there. It is very difficult to accurately guage the size of rooms when a house is empty. Ironically, homes and individual rooms look larger when they are furnished.

Even if you have your home partially staged or revamped, it could make the difference between attracting one interested party or quickly receiving multiple offers.

The idea is to make each living space reveal an example of its particular lifestyle for prospective buyers. It is so helpful to buyers to be able to see themselves living in the property.

Readying your home for the market, putting it in its best light (literally as well as figuratively) may take 3-4 weeks. If you are planning a move or are planning on selling your home or any of your properties you may want to consult an expert to get a professional recommendation – someone with a "buyer's eye" as I like to call it. You can then allot the time and cost for those items or for those areas of your home you choose to "freshen up" or completely revamp, such as painting a room or two.

In some cases, this way you can practically "schedule" your sale and move. This market is one of the rare times in which you can almost orchestrate the whole thing from start to finish. That is a secure feeling if you are a seller.

Another recommended preparation, which is prudent for you in the long run, is to do your own property inspections beforehand so that you can make adjustments for either repairs or to the pricing.

The January 2015 Scott Report — 4th Quarter 2014 Summary
Beverly Hills Real Estate Facts, Values, Trends and Opportunities for Homeowners and Buyers

For instance, if you've never had the sewer line or the foundation inspected, you may want to have those items inspected to save any surprises (for both you and the buyer). Up front is the best and most ethical way to do business when selling.

Also a termite/wood destroying pest report. Mold inspection. Chimney inspection. These inspections are fairly standard today, and are up to the buyer to order and pay for. Usually it's at the buyer's request, and customarily the buyer pays for his due diligence (inspections), but if you can have them done (and can afford to) beforehand it may save you in the long run.

It will also give you a realistic and more in-depth understanding of your own property. Even if you don't intend to do any of the repairs, disclosing these conditions up-front will help a buyer to close escrow in spite of conditions instead of back away while discovering anything during the escrow.

The way to maximize your profits right now is to get your home "showroom" ready, or as close to it as you can. Sometimes that can mean something as simple as removing your personal articles from the home – family photos, clearing any portable electronics, laptop computers, etc. Or, although more extensive, it can be repainting the whole interior and re-doing all of the flooring depending on what you think your home needs to make it most appealing for prospective buyers.

It could be "freshening-up" the kids' bedrooms who have moved off to college 5 years ago. Make repairs to minor things in your home that should be operational such as any of the built-in kitchen appliances and replacing burnt out light bulbs.

As active as today's market is, it is forcing buyers to make very quick buying decisions. Therefore, I would say a big key to these times, that shouldn't be rushed, are your seller disclosures. As a seller, be very thorough on your disclosures. Your agent can help you while filling out the forms. This is the time for your "ounce of prevention." It shouldn't be rushed, or worse, taken too casually. If you're selling, this step could prove pivotal.

For instance, when the market begins to level off before changing to a down turn, as it is this quarter, now is the height of the market. Buyer's feel compelled to make quick decisions, and they may (and I emphasize *may*) look for compensation to offset the (perceived) premiums paid during these times.

Therefore, I advise my clients to be thorough on disclosures, using the Seller Property Questionnaire and Buyer's Transfer Disclosure Statement (mandatory documents in all residential sales) as merely a guideline, and then disclose *anything* else over and above. This forces an "eyes wide open" transaction that won't have repercussions down the line, sometimes years after the escrow has closed.

Even the nicest buyer, may have a lawyer hiding somewhere in their family tree, and over an Easter brunch 3 years after the sale that same buyer might be lamenting about something regarding the property that isn't functioning right, or even a chronic problem that has surfaced since they moved into the house, and immediately they could suspect the prior seller (you) of having the same problem and not disclosing it.

That super nice buyer who bought your home in the peak of the market, who felt the pressure to make an immediate decision for fear they may have lost the house, and might have paid more than he ideally wished to, could feel justified in coming back to you (the seller) for financial compensation.

> "As active as today's market is, it is forcing buyers to make very quick decisions."

The January 2015 Scott Report — 4th Quarter 2014 Summary
BEVERLY HILLS REAL ESTATE FACTS, VALUES, TRENDS AND OPPORTUNITIES FOR HOMEOWNERS AND BUYERS

So, perhaps particularly in this market, SELLER BEWARE! Just make sure to cross all of your T's and double dot your I's and have your agent do the same. A good and thorough agent will guide you through the paperwork. It is straight-forward but important.

That you should expect of the agent you choose. I recommend you do some research. Call an escrow company for a reference on the agent you'll be using to represent you and see how "clean" their escrows are. How accurate the paperwork is. How solution oriented they are.

Does the agent you are considering have the resources to solve an unexpected problem (i.e. a cloud on your title that you weren't aware was there that would delay or even forbear the sale)?

It is always worth choosing your agent wisely. Even though you happen to know someone with a real estate license, it may be a sound investment to add a solid agent to the team, or just choose a solid agent from the start. After all, business is business; business is not emotional or personal. But it certainly can affect you personally if something comes back to bite due to careless representation, not to mention unnecessary stress and delay during your sale or purchase process.

Representation is a combination of:

1. Accuracy in all documentation. A good agent will have a thorough knowledge of all of the documents and contracts that are used in a transaction. If there are other issues such as permits or zoning ordinances, that agent should know where to obtain the information, not necessarily be schooled on it, but at least know where to find it for your particular transaction.

> "I advise all sellers to be thorough with disclosures. This forces an 'eyes-wide-open transaction that will not have later repercussions."

2. Marketing. This should really be tied with number 1. Marketing as I define it is ethically yet powerfully exposing your property to as many targeted clients as possible. This can and should be done daily, creatively and pro-actively.

The Multiple Listing Service "MLS" which exposes your property to the other agents in the industry is really a communication tool, it doesn't target the market nor market to agents or buyers directly. It is more of an information source.

Yes, all agents who are members of the MLS have access to the same information, but good, knowledgeable and ethical agents *sell* your home and *protect you* from potential legal potholes. Neither the MLS nor the internet sells your home or protects you during the sale. The MLS and websites are nothing more than information sources.

Let's say you are selling your home in today's low inventory market, and let's say you have received no offers after it has been on the market for 30 days. You ask you agent what to do.

If the agent first answers, "price reduction" he or she may not be proactively marketing your home, or may not know how best to. There are very specific, tested methods of marketing specific categories of home. If your agent does not know this, your home, firstly, is less likely to be exposed to the highest numbers of serious and qualified prospective buyers, and secondly, it may be a casualty of a too early price reduction.

Price reduction attacks your bottom line. You leave pure profit on the table. If you have been diligent about accurately pricing your home, price reduction is not always the solution. In fact, it is often the last move to make. I would much rather be in a negotiation and have a qualified buyer ask for a price reduction, than a listing

The January 2015 Scott Report — 4th Quarter 2014 Summary
Beverly Hills Real Estate Facts, Values, Trends and Opportunities for Homeowners and Buyers

agent with no buyer and no prospective buyer ask for profit reduction, especially if it's before they have done everything in their power to market the property (unless it's been unintentionally over-priced).

And I'm not just talking about two or three open houses, I'm talking about proactive, ongoing marketing until your home sells. The goal of marketing is to get the information out to as many targeted buyers as possibly, intelligently and consistently, while representing the property ethically.

3. An aspect of a good agent is his or her availability, hospitality and professionalism. Your agent should be naturally warm and welcoming. He or she should be attentive to you, clients and colleagues alike.

They should work with you and the interested party, making the times flexible and convenient for both. They should make any and all requested information about your house readily available.

Your agent should have good relationships with other agents in the community where your property is located. They will be allying with them and their clients to accomplish your goals.

In essence, you, the seller, will be relying on the prospective buyer's agent via your agent. Every agent is, at the end of the day, still working for the seller, even when he or she is representing a buyer.

Also make sure your agent is aware of your goals. Your agent should share your game plan. Your mutual goals should be to ethically achieve the highest market value price, acceptable terms (escrow periods, possession) with enough explanation and enough preparation for you to make you feel confident with the sale of your home, the pace of that sale, and also with the resources your agent makes available to you to meet any situation that may come up during the course of the sale, and your subsequent purchase of a new home (if you are also buying a home).

If You Are Buying

If you are a buyer, one thing is still certain in this 3rd Quarter 2014 which is still a seller's market: you need to be decisive and quite fast-acting.

Maybe surprisingly, there are wonderful opportunities for buyers in this booming market. Yes, inventory is low but because it's a seller's market, long term residents are motivated to sell homes that have not been available for up to 20, 30 or 40 years or more.

A combination of good, exceptional and sometimes rare buying opportunities are becoming available almost weekly, and because Beverly Hills has a fixed number of lots (which will never increase) both lot and home values are always rising.

Being well prepared with the ability to act fast is my advice – particularly in this market. There are no guarantees of course, because at least two more potential buyers will be seeking the same house you are interested in. But having the ability to act fast with solid preparation behind you will give you the best chance at winning the property you really want.

Physically prepare by looking at property. Always get out into the marketplace. Get a fresh feel for houses, lot sizes, streets and values. Looking online only counts

> "If your agent first answers, 'price reduction,' he or she may not be proactively marketing your home, or may not know how most effectively to."

The January 2015 Scott Report — 4th Quarter 2014 Summary
Beverly Hills Real Estate Facts, Values, Trends and Opportunities for Homeowners and Buyers

partially. The only way to establish your sense of today's values – which as you know are quickly appreciating – is to physically see and feel the variations that make up home pricing and value.

This way when you find the property you want to make an offer on, and really feel that you want to go all the way with it, you'll just 'know' it's the right deal and have the extra confidence in your decision. *Internet real estate sites advertise price. You, your agent and the market ultimately determine the value.*

Sometimes I walk into a house for sale and I know it's going to be worth more even by the time it closes escrow. Its charm or striking design or location or all three tell me its value will increase rapidly. And that is a rarity.

If I don't have an exact buyer for it, I still wish I could be the one to give this "gift" to someone who will feel the same way I do in that moment. It feels as if I've found a genuine piece of art at a garage sale! It is the same as when you're in the entertainment business, just knowing when you happen on real, undiscovered talent. Your heart begins to pound because you know you're onto something, sometimes it's even before the rest of the world finds out.

You will begin to get this same feel for a home the more property you visit. Most buyers do not do enough leg-work. When you do, you gain a real advantage in the market – a sixth sense. And that's what you want with you to house-hunt.

At least you can do that to prepare as a buyer in this competitive market. First of all, let me say that if you haven't yet been in a bidding war for a property – 3-10 offers or more – consider yourself lucky! Many buyers are challenged with the prospect of searching furiously on the internet for new listings as they hit the market, or they have an agent who gets a jump on the public by knowing of an "off market" house for sale before it is officially made public. This scenario can feel urgent and futile all at the same time. But there is good news.

This is when having solid representation is well worth the agent fee (as opposed to going it alone or with a with a discount or rebate-offering agency.

I encourage you to write the offer as cleanly as possible. Write the most flexible terms and full asking price if there are multiple offers. If your agent has done his or her homework, they have asked the listing agent "what terms are your sellers looking for?" And you write your offer as closely to those terms as possible, if not those exact terms if they also suit you.

Remember the listing price is the seller's offer to the public. In essence, *your* offer is a response to their offer.

Include in your offer package some facts about you. Ask yourself, are there any particular facts about you or your circumstance that would inspire the seller to be on your side? Include your bank statement and down payment monies. I have my clients shoot a short video on their smart phone. It really helps the seller see into the person and the deal rather than having just a name and an offer on a form.

You'll know soon enough if there will be multiple offers (these are the times we are in; lots of cash buyers who have pulled their investments out of the unpredictable stock market and are investing in the quickly appreciating California (both Northern and Southern) real estate market.

Also, lenders have loosened up after the bail out, so

> "Internet real estate sites only advertise price. You, your agent and the market ultimately determine the real and optimal value."

banks are lending a little more fluidly. Inventory (the number of homes on the market) is still relatively low; low supply and high demand. Now is the time to be over-prepared, to be competitive, to win the house you really love and want to own.

Get yourself pre-approved for a mortgage, contingent on the appraisal of the house you choose. Luckily everything you'll need to be competitive is at your fingertips!

Buying decisions are sometimes made on the spot. I've witnessed it! Because of that, I recommend looking at a lot of property mainly to establish value, so when 'the one' comes your way, you'll feel as if you will do everything in your power to win the bidding war – and it will be worth it. It usually is.

Be prepared financially. Get all of the information that affects every dollar involved. Talk with your accountants about the tax benefits of your move. Talk with your mortgage broker /banker about dollars and cents. "How much exactly will I pay, do I qualify for, will my dollar buy?"

Preparation will give you greater confidence, which gives any seller you make an offer to greater confidence to enter into a transaction with you.

In this market, you need every edge. You can make yourself almost as strong as the "all cash" buyer by having all the facts and figures researched before you submit your offer. The marketplace is competitive for buyers, yet in these ways, you can make yourself stand out to a seller.

In order to get in on the quickly appreciating real estate market, speak to a mortgage broker or your bank about qualifying for a loan (if you intend to apply for a mortgage for your purchase).

The lender can pre-approve you contingent on appraisal, rather than merely issue a pre-qualification letter. Pre-qualification merely means they've checked your credit score and you would qualify for a certain loan amount (one of the various loan products, from the conservative 30 year fixed to the more risky interest only products – 5 year, 7 year and 10 year).

A pre-approval letter shows you have submitted all of the documentation as if you're in escrow applying for the loan. Your lender will need job and housing history as well as income and asset verification. The lender proceeds to submit your loan package to underwriting who make the final decision on the approval, contingent on appraisal.

After that is completed, or at least started, you as a borrower are armed with so many options that when it comes to making your offer and purchasing, you will have less surprises and you will come across as one of the strongest offer because your representative will communicate that you have come "prepared to close"!!

Another option is open to you if you intend to have a mortgage on the property but you also have the cash to pay the full amount for it. You can offer "all cash" and then apply for a purchase money (as opposed to a re-finance) mortgage up to 90 days after the close of escrow and still qualify, for the same rates as if you were applying during escrow (unless rates increase during the time).

In this way, you can be more attractive to a seller if you need to be.

> "Be financially prepared. Get all the information that affects every dollar involved. Talk to your accountant about the tax benefits of your move."

The January 2015 Scott Report — 4th Quarter 2014 Summary
Beverly Hills Real Estate Facts, Values, Trends and Opportunities for Homeowners and Buyers

There are a few factors involved in being able to win a bidding war if it comes down to it. One, of course, is the price you offer; the other is the listing agent. Do they feel *your* agent is expert and easy to do business with? Believe it or not, this may influence who wins the house. The listing agent wants to have confidence in your agent. Remember, the listing agent has one goal in mind – to close the transaction on behalf of the seller with the most acceptable deal possible.

Is your agent a 'brother-in-law' who happens to have a real estate license and is "representing" you because you are trying to help a family member out? Maybe not in your overall best interest.

Choose your agent wisely. When it comes to submitting your offer, representing you in a way that is most appealing to the particular seller and agent, and protecting you and your investment, it is worth it. Good representation certainly factors in when it comes to winning a bidding war.

Also, remember, even though the seller is selling and moving, on some level he wants his home to go to someone who will take good care of it. To some sellers there is a sentimental attachment to their home even though they're selling and moving on. They like the new buyer to have a certain sentiment towards the house as well. This can factor in if they have to choose between two or more buyers.

Most of all they're looking to chose the buyer who fully intends to close with the most acceptable terms. A good agent knows how to present this well to a seller's agent.

It is stressful for the buyer before he or she enters into escrow. The selection process and then the (multiple) offer process are anticipatory.

But then it becomes a stressful ride for the seller after escrow opens. That's why he will ultimately chose a buyer who "fully intends to close." Mostly before all of the contingencies (buyer's legal outs) have been removed, the seller feels the tension the whole way.

So if your agent has sufficiently and expertly conveyed your intentions, and your intentions are earnest and your supporting factors are solid it will make it easier for the seller to choose your offer over others. Even if this were a "normal" market, all of these things would still be important, but now more than ever, they are essential.

If You Are Selling and Buying at The Same Time

(and if you want or need to sell before you buy)

If your equity is tied up in your current home and you need it for the down payment on your new home, don't worry! Some fall into this category. Here is a solution that contains little risk and the freedom for you to find, secure and then buy your new home.

As a buyer, what can you do? To add to the frenzy, you need to sell your current property to move up or across or to down-size. Now what? You are in limbo.

There is a new advent. Always where there is challenge, there is opportunity. Here's how it works:

There is a provision known as a Contingency of Sale or Purchase for buyers – making an offer on a house with a proviso that the buyer's

> "The lender can pre-approve you contingent on appraisal, rather than merely issue a pre-qualification letter."

current house sells as the buyer is relying on equity from their current home to use as the down payment on their new home.

In this market, a seller's market, the number of homes for sale are still low, so while it is relatively certain your home will sell quickly if priced well, and before the market turns (when sales become more sluggish), this is the time for a seller to use the transitional sale or contingency listing – making the listing and negotiated sale subject to seller finding suitable housing. You list your home with the provision of securing your new home as a condition of the sale up front.

As more inventory (choices) are introduced in the market, you as the buyer can feel more confident in selecting a home and moving forward with confidence.

You have a little more time to decide on the right place to buy with a greater selection. Then all that's necessary is orchestrating your move(s). Win-win-win.

I think now is the time to utilize this method if you need to sell in order to buy. If your agent hasn't already suggested it, ask him or her about it – the benefits and drawbacks, and whether it is right for you.

Here's an example of how it works: Let's say you have a property worth between 2 million to 7 million dollars. You definitely want to sell, but you'll sell only if you have a place in which to move. Whether you need the equity from your current house, or you just don't want to carry two homes, you want or need to sell and buy at the same time. Apart from anything else, if you can avoid moving twice, you'd prefer to. You want to avoid renting a property after you've sold your home while you shop for your new home. One, clean move is what you prefer, and I agree!

In this case, you can offer your home for sale. Pull out all of the stops, get it ready for prospective buyers to see. Have its photo shoot, write the smartest brochure, a piece that highlights the emotion of your home as well as its physical attributes and dimensions.

I have discovered that, interestingly enough, a buyer is often like the seller in many ways and is often attracted to the property for similar reasons, both physically and emotionally. So showing your home with all its dimension is certainly advantageous.

When all of this choreographed preparation is done, your home is introduced to the marketplace in it's most flattering and realistic light.

First it's announced to the Real Estate industry in the Multiple Listing Service (MLS). The MLS listing instantly reaches 14,000 local agents who pass the details onto interested potential buyers.

(Note that if you list your house with a Coldwell Banker agent such as Victoria Scott Estates, Inc or any other, your home details are automatically placed on more than 600 real estate and real estate related websites worldwide. This is usually the most effective and fastest way of attracting the right buyer. Some sellers wish to remain private. If so, there are more discreet,

> " When your agent sufficiently and expertly conveys your intentions, and your intentions are earnest and your supporting factors are solid, it makes it easier for the seller to choose your offer over others. "

> " Your home for sale instantly reaches hundreds of potential buyers through Coldwell Banker's 600+ affiliated, specialist web sites. "

The January 2015 Scott Report — 4th Quarter 2014 Summary
Beverly Hills Real Estate Facts, Values, Trends and Opportunities for Homeowners and Buyers

yet still effective ways to market the property.)

When you list your property and are using the equity to purchase another property, a contingency clause allows you to sell your home *only* when you've secured a new property. If you have not found a new property, you as the seller can cancel the sale within a designated and agreed to time period. Everything about this contingency is up front, transparent, and in good faith. This is a calculated risk for all, but done with ethical communication and slight flexibility, it serves the needs of this current market and reduces the risk enough to make the transition less daunting for a seller if you need to sell in order to buy. It can also buy time for a buyer in a similar situation.

If the buyer you procure is an all cash buyer, there is an opportunity for you to stay in your home for up to (and in some cases beyond) 60 days after the close of escrow. I've seen this extended period cost as little as one dollar per month for the person staying on.

The listing agreement will have a Contingency of Purchase (COP) designating how much time (while in escrow) you, the seller has to enter into another escrow and secure your purchase. This is a negotiable length of time, most likely between 17-30 days. It can run concurrent with the new buyers' contingency periods. These time periods are negotiable and agreed upon by both buyer and seller.

Remember, in some cases you are just looking for yours and your buyers' situations to line up.

Also, a lease back for 30 days can be set up after your current home closes escrow. This allows you to remain in the property for up to 30 days after the closing for a set dollar amount (sometimes $1 as mentioned above)

> *"If your buyer is an all-cash buyer, there is an opportunity for you to stay in your home for up to—and in some cases beyond—60 days after the close of escrow."*

so that you can make all of the final preparations to close escrow on your new property, secure the cash coming from the sale of your current home, and move comfortably.

All times frames are in writing, and agreed to by both parties. There is no set formula, it is just a case of buyer and seller agreeing.

Longer escrow periods or contingency periods where needed, are up for discussion, and as long as both parties agree, are considered good and ethical business.

The response will be typical (a lot of interest if the property is priced well) apart from any prospective buyers who find too much uncertainty in purchasing a home that has a Contingency clause protecting the seller. This buyer will typically bow out.

In this market, you will quickly discover your home's market value, therefore then be able to make decisions based on exact dollar amounts. This makes a Contingency listing a low-risk way to market and sell your home. And if your situation demands it, it allows you to get into the market place sooner rather than later.

The Ethics of Buying and Selling Real Estate

Always enter into a transaction in good faith. Good faith is doing business honestly with the intention to honor everything that you've signed or agreed to. Always sell or purchase a home with as much revealed information as possible. That way there are no unwitting or hidden surprises.

We always respect the process and all parties in-

The January 2015 Scott Report — 4th Quarter 2014 Summary
BEVERLY HILLS REAL ESTATE FACTS, VALUES, TRENDS AND OPPORTUNITIES FOR HOMEOWNERS AND BUYERS

volved. If you feel as if you need additional support, more than you receive from your agent and their brokerage, consider adding an accountant or an attorney to counsel you – not to complicate the transaction, but to simplify it and give you a greater sense of having "eyes wide open" and reassurance.

It is almost impossible to know every variable in certain cases. Many times, just when I think I've seen it all, something new pops up. But having the intention to do business honestly and transparently smoothes out most if not all surprises to end with equitable results.

Ethics and transparency are always the best way of doing business. In any business this is true, and it is certainly true in real estate especially when many sellers and buyers are feeling the heat of the booming market. I like being an open book. Earnestness and transparency is the ethical way of business today.

After all, who cannot make a good decision knowing all the facts and that all parties involved are honorable.

The January 2015 Scott Report — 4th Quarter 2014 Summary
Beverly Hills Real Estate Facts, Values, Trends and Opportunities for Homeowners and Buyers

Sage and Timely Real Estate Advice From Industry Veteran, Stan Richman

To glean information from Beverly Hills real estate veteran, Stan Richman, is rare for most residents. Stan runs the Beverly Hills North office of Coldwell Banker, the USA's number 1 real estate company. He shares wisdom and timely advice for all who are planning to sell or buy today.

Stan Richman, Manager/VP
Coldwell Banker Beverly Hills
North Office

A Little Background, and Three Big Changes In The Beverly Hills Market In The Last 35 Years

I started out as an agent in 1979 with Jon Douglas company and then was with Jon Douglas until he was sold to Coldwell Banker in 1997. So I've been with Coldwell Banker since 1997. There have been some big changes in the market during these 35 years.

The number one change is price. Our prices are five times what where they were when I first started, maybe more in some areas. We never would have thought a property [let's say] in the 500 block of flats which, when I my first got in the business, was $900,000, would now be 4 to 5 million. So you can see that that is 4 to 5 times multiple since 1980, the change in the marketplace.

We have had cycles between that, where it has gone up-and-down. But holding [onto property] is part of real estate, so if you hold, it usually always comes back.

Cycles peak in the city as opposed to other areas. Some of the outlying areas, like Pasadena, for instance, wouldn't have the great ups but wouldn't have the great downs either because it's somewhat of a conservative area and prices are way up there. But in the early 90s Beverly Hills went down maybe 40% whereas Pasadena maybe went down 10 to 20%. Then when we went up, we went up above the 40 to maybe 100 percent above that. So the city peaks and troughs more severly which is good for most people. It's the holding. Whoever holds benefits from it. If you have to sell during a bad cycle it's a problem.

The second change is the Internet. The Internet has changed how we do business. The consumer now probably knows as much about the business as we do. Internet advertising probably dominates how we sell homes. It [itself] will never sell homes of course, because, luckily in LA it's different, but that has changed everything, how we write contracts, how we sell homes, how we present properties, how we market ourselves, and how we market properties.

The greatest benefit of the internet to the homeowner is that he and she is now much more knowledgeable. That's the bottom line. They used to know because they saw sign up for a house for sale, or a house sold. Now they have access, between all the sites, to know what sold, when, how long ago. They know as much as most realtors do.

The more informed the client is, the better it is for the whole industry because we can deal with clients on a much more professional basis. Instead of having to explain over and over again the situation with any particular property, we can explain once on our web

The January 2015 Scott Report — 4th Quarter 2014 Summary
Beverly Hills Real Estate Facts, Values, Trends and Opportunities for Homeowners and Buyers

site. Then everyone knows about the property. Some people don't use or like the Internet that much, but 75% of buyers and sellers use it and know what's going on in the marketplace.

There are good and bad things about the Internet. There are so many sites, for instance like Zillow, that will sometimes list a price range that clients think their house is worth, but it can be 30% off. So clients look at that and they think their house is worth 'X' and maybe it's not. So, that has changed the client's perspective somewhat. The consumer doesn't necessarily really realize that a stated price on Zillow doesn't mean their property is going to sell for that amount of money. Sometimes that's a rude awakening. Other times it's better because sometimes their sells for more than they're thinking it should sell for.

The only other negative is that when you put your house up for sale on the Internet everybody knows about it. There's no privacy. So you have to be prepared for that kind of scenario in your life. That's what we've got to do, is be able to tell the sellers that once it's out it's out. That's our job.

A really good thing about the internet is being able to get property details out there. That's why everything should be listed through the Multiple Listing Service where it goes onto all of our affiliated websites. It is exposed to the most amount of people because that's the best and highest way to get your price. That's sometimes the fallacy of pocket [non-publicly listed] listings. Some people just don't want the invasion of people in their home, but I think they're always leaving something on the table if they don't [list their property on the MLS].

The third change is the amount of companies and the number of agents. The amount of agents, from when I first started, are probably one hundred percent more, maybe as much as two hundred percent more. So the competitive nature of the marketplace has changed. It is what it is. Companies have changed — different companies to do things differently.

The increased number of agents and agencies has increased the professionalism offered to the client because there is a different standard. But there are always people that will, I'm afraid, lower those standards too.

There are so many agents and only so much property. Some consumers don't do their job by really looking at whom they're dealing with. That is a problem.

The increased competitive nature of the industry keeps pushing up the standard of the best companies — the companies that are always seeking ways to innovate and improve. That's the mantra of our company. For instance, on the street we're known as the training company. We have the best training. We have been involved in training since the beginning here.

We have more people involved in training and doing the right thing and basically knowing the fiduciary we have to the buyer and seller. I don't know if that's even done in a lot of companies and that's the sad part. So the standard isn't always the same company versus company. We try to communicate that to the consumer but a lot of times other things are playing a part. I've never understood that. You're selling your biggest asset, why wouldn't you do as much due diligence as you can to find out who you are getting involved with, because whether it's a friend or a relative you know, we're talking about millions and millions of dollars these days.

> *"There are always agents who will, I am afraid, lower those standards too."*

> *"There are good and bad things about the Internet. Many sites, for instance Zillow, list a price range that can be 30% off… (so) the more informed the client is, the better."*

The January 2015 Scott Report — 4th Quarter 2014 Summary
BEVERLY HILLS REAL ESTATE FACTS, VALUES, TRENDS AND OPPORTUNITIES FOR HOMEOWNERS AND BUYERS

SHORTAGE OF PROPERTIES FOR SALE TODAY

Today, there is a shortage of properties available for sale. We've had a very strong market – this is the fourth year in Beverly Hills. So I think the growth in the westside of L.A. – and not just the westside, could be Pasadena, La Canada, the Asian market out there, the Palisades, certain areas like the whole west side, – the growth is there because the amount of people with money has changed dramatically in L.A. Never in my lifetime, and I was born and raised here, have I seen so many people with money come to L.A., and of all nationalities. It used to be true of New York, now we're seeing it, for the last 5 to 10 years, here. And that has changed the scope of how many people want to live here.

One reason they come here is for security. They feel safe here in Beverly Hills. It's no longer just the schools, it's the best fire, the best police. You know, they feel very comfortable here compared to other places. We have a lot of people from all parts of the world that will build a home and visit once in a while and maybe come for one day or one or two weeks. So we have a lot of homes that are used a third of the year or two thirds of the year. We've never had that in the past.

The Asian marketplace has changed real estate, dramatically. We're seeing it mostly in the San Gabriel Valley and we're seeing it a little bit here, especially in the high-end numbers. It hasn't become as expensive as Manhattan, but it's getting there. To live on the westside you really have to be fairly well-off. 25 years ago that wasn't the case.

There are a number of contributing factors to the shortage of homes available for sale. I think what we've just had last year, was a giant boom year. We did more volume than we've ever done. The year before we did a lot of volume too. I think there just aren't a lot of builders. We have some – spec builders coming on the market. It's expensive to buy, therefore they're not doing as many as they have in the past, say in the late 80s, when it was pretty cheap to buy.

Also people are staying in their homes longer. We have a lot of people that just live their whole lives in the one home. They don't move out. They don't go into a condo. They're well off enough to have help at home and just wait for whatever happens. So that's changed that, in that respect. There's not one particular reason for the shortage of homes. Because our company is nationwide, we talk about every city. And in every city, right now, they have the same shortage. Miami's got the same, Chicago's got the same, Manhattan's the same, so are all the major cities, practically. There are just not enough homes being built. We had a slow down, for five years, where not a lot of people built. When you do that it takes time for things to catch up. It will be another two or three quarters, or maybe another year, before we get normal inventory.

> "The increased competitive nature of the industry keeps pushing up the standard of the best real estates companies."

Builders and developers have an impact on this market. In the 1 to 3 million dollar range as a buy, they're having a big impact, because they're buying for lot value, wanting to build. Some builders have about 18-20 projects going in that price range and those deals are for all cash. When they make their offer they are willing to take it non-contingent.

In the bigger stuff too, as well as the view properties, there are a lot of builders out there. We just don't have enough to sell. They're trying to buy and build big, big and with views, for resale. Also for some owner-users as well. It's about a 60% owner-user, 40% spec builder.

Flippers? It's pretty hard to be a flipper because the

costs are so much, but there are some, definitely. It's not a major part; building new is the major part. New really gets top price. New in every area will get 20% more than a remodeled house. In Cheviot Hills we just broke a record for 4.7 million for a new house. They've never seen that kind of dollar.

There is also a change in home style preference, for contemporary-style homes. We never have had such a demand for contemporary homes and yet California, the Westside, lends itself to that type of living. People in the entertainment industry really, mostly, want contemporary. They want a contemporary type of lifestyle. So you get trends. Right now might be a hard time selling English style homes, you know, the type that are darker, with lots of wood. Whereas those styles would have sold more easily when I first got in the business over 25 years ago – the charming style, with small rooms. No one wants small rooms, they still want charm but with big rooms. So that's a big change, from older to contemporary, with that contemporary lifestyle. Everyone wants offices. Everybody wants a room for their theater, whether small or large that they want some place to watch big-screen TVs. And they want indoor-outdoor living. It's changed in these ways.

Advantages If You Are Selling In This Market

If a person is considering selling their home in this market, there are some advantages in doing it now as opposed to, say, a year from now because we never know what a year from now is going to bring. You know, we always take a bird in the hand, taking into account what's happening currently. You've got a strong market with low rates and you've got a lot of demand, so why, if you are going to move soon anyway, wouldn't you put your house on the market with all those things in your favor? Whereas, next year, God forbid we have an earthquake or something happens. Life, you know, can change in a year.

So, to me, it's like waiting for stock to peak out. If you start waiting for the top, by the time you sell it, you lose. It's the same thing in this business. I look at all of the numbers every month because it really speaks to where we're going. You can just tell month-by-month.

> "If a person is considering selling their home in this market, there are some advantages in doing it now as opposed to, say, a year from now."

If someone is considering selling their home right now, there are a few things that will really help them. First, really examine who you are getting involved with, the agent as well as the company. I would really do that. That to me is a priority.

Pricing is really important, too. Make sure you are thoroughly understanding the pricing. And take an objective look at your house. Understand the little things that you can do, like paint and other minor things to make it fresh and newer, things people take for granted like landscaping. Do little things that don't cost a lot of money.

You should also look at a lot of new property you may be interested in as your new home. If you're going to sell you should really know where you are going to go. So I think that's important. At least have an idea, so at least you can take the strong offer and move on with it.

If a seller doesn't have a place to go or can't find a place to buy, then they should, first of all, be looking where they might go, and then maybe structure in a leaseback for 60 days or something, where it gives them more time.

The key is the willingness of the seller to want to

The January 2015 Scott Report — 4th Quarter 2014 Summary
BEVERLY HILLS REAL ESTATE FACTS, VALUES, TRENDS AND OPPORTUNITIES FOR HOMEOWNERS AND BUYERS

sell. If they really want to sell, this is the time to do it. But if you're afraid of the next step, I don't know, this market is little tough for that, so you better be prepared to have alternatives in mind – of where you can move. Or you might want to lease a place for a year after you sell. You should have some option that is your next step. Because you're probably going to get that one offer you can't refuse and you've got to be willing to take it.

If you were a buyer in this low inventory market, first of all find the right agent because they're going to be the one that gets you in front of, hopefully, the right property at the right time. Choose an agent who is not too busy, you know, who doesn't have 1000 listings! I've never understood why people get involved with an agent who has 25 listings. You need to have someone who can pay some attention to you. Also, be realistic about what you want to pay. Make sure you're qualified with the lenders quickly, so you can move fast. Just know where you have options. Have more than one option about where you want to live.

> "One mistake I see seller's repeatedly make is accepting the first highest offer, but not the strongest."

One mistake I see sellers repeatedly make is getting involved with the first highest offer, but with not really the strongest person in the deal. So, for instance, a deal that has long contingency periods and maybe not enough cash down, and just going for the price. That's the number one thing sellers really get in trouble with. We've discovered that sometimes the highest price does have the best terms, but the key in this market is to get it closed as quickly as you can.

One thing I would love to be able to advise all sellers about, to avoid a lot of problems, is to know their property and to do their due diligence. We recommend to people, if they're living in an older house and they've never looked at, for instance, the sewer system, which has been there 40 years, and then all of a sudden they've got someone in a deal and the sewer system is bad, and it needs a whole new sewer pipe which can be really expensive, to check things like this first – those unknown things that all of a sudden come up. Where the seller's aghast that the costs are so much to keep the deal.

That's the number one thing. That's why, for instance, we really want people to get a termite report beforehand, just to know the condition of their property. Even though they think they know, sometimes they don't know.

On big properties, it is worth the seller investing in doing some due diligence before they put it up for sale. Especially sewer systems. The seller should be having someone video the sewer system to know what condition it's in.

For the seller's sake, hopefully, they don't have mold. If they do, that should be remedied before they put it on the market. That scares a lot of people, things like that. If you've got leaks, just to take care of those things will help to ensure an offer doesn't fall apart. Hopefully people have the wherewithal to do things like this before they put their property on the market.

Then there is seller's frustration during escrow. For instance, loans are taking longer, and the frustration of, sometimes, the closing being delayed a week or two. Or there's something that happens that extends the original escrow period. That's the obligation of a good listing broker to say, "Look, things can happen. Just because we have an april 1st intended closing doesn't mean you'll actually close on that exact date." The banks are all running late and the frustration level gets really, incredibly, difficult at times. We deal with so many different people. Some people look at dates

The January 2015 Scott Report — 4th Quarter 2014 Summary
Beverly Hills Real Estate Facts, Values, Trends and Opportunities for Homeowners and Buyers

and run by those dates, whereas other people disregard those dates. You've just got to be careful how you treat dates.

Investing in the Beverly Hills area? We don't sell residential strictly as an investment. We still look at it as consumer based, that buyers are going to live there. Our job is not to sell investments. And I really look at it that way. You know, it's a lifestyle, that's what I think. We sell homes for lifestyle, not usually for investment. If you hold onto property in Beverly Hills, if you graft out the ups and downs, the prices have always, sooner or later, gone up.

There are other things that make this city so appealing, and give it a unique lifestyle. It's a feeling. It's a small city. People feel very comfortable here. The restaurants, the lifestyle, and a feeling of knowing who your neighbor is. It's so multinational that you feel like you can be part of any segment. It's really grown in so many different areas.

THE NEXT 6 MONTHS

In the next 6 months I think we're going to see more of the same – multiple offers on a lot of properties that are priced well. If you're overpriced by 10-15% in some areas, it's not going to sell. So within two weeks we can know if it's salable or not salable, if it's close or not close. I think we're going to see more of the same. We have cheap money, which is good, although it's still tough to get loans all the time, which isn't making things that much easier. There's still a lot of cash around, which is good.

In a year, I think the same. In two years, I've no idea. What you can't do is look back to see some kind of reliable pattern. Never. In 1989 it was a boom year for me, I was still selling at that time. Then in 1990 everything changed, especially the high-end which went down 80% in sales. 1991-94 was even worse with the riots and the earthquake. So for four years we didn't have a lot of business. None of us expected it, but it sure happened. Then we grew out of it in 1995, and 1996 things started to get strong. 1997 onwards things were strong. We had a little lull in the early 2000's and we grew out of it again.

So it's those kinds of cycles. I think it hasn't hit us really hard since the early 90s. That really hit hard here. It hurt a lot of other areas in 2000, with high foreclosure rates. But all those areas have come back – Las Vegas, has come back; Arizona's come back.

THERE IS SOMETHING HAPPENING CURRENTLY THAT HASN'T BEEN SEEN BEFORE

There is something happening currently that really hasn't been seen before. View properties have become and are making a bigger impact in the marketplace than I've ever seen. They were always desired but I think there's something additional that is happening.

I think the foreign buyers really love the idea of coming to L.A. And having a view. Also people in entertainment like having a view. So there's a multitude of different factors that change the feel, and when it becomes popular, like anything else, it becomes very popular. People with money, if they decide they want something, they want

> "One thing I would love to advise all sellers about, to avoid problems and delays, is to know their property and to do their due diligence."

The January 2015 Scott Report — 4th Quarter 2014 Summary
Beverly Hills Real Estate Facts, Values, Trends and Opportunities for Homeowners and Buyers

what they want, and they'll pay for it.

Some sellers are seeing 13, 14 offers on their homes but we've had that before. In the late 90s we had it like that, multiple offers on properties. In the late 80s, the same conditions, seller's expecting multiple offers. But the popularity of view properties is a new aspect right now, and the amount in cash is also new. We've never had this many cash offers. It's unheard of. The amount of people that are coming here are wealthy. Cash is something that's prevalent in the baby boomer generation, which really makes up a lot of the movement we've had, and their kids have inherited a lot of money. We've never had inheritance in L.A. like we have now. That's a thing that New York has always had, and Europe always has had. But we've never had it in L.A.

And now we've seen people, people I know, people in the marketplace who have inherited giant sums of money. That's what they're doing, buying properties. Trust funds, amounts that we've never seen before. The baby boomers themselves, if they haven't retired, they've sold out or something. So, for a lot of them across the board, they've accumulated a lot of cash.

> "There are other things that make Beverly Hills so appealing and give it its unique lifestyle."

3 MOST IMPORTANT THINGS

Be careful who you get into bed with. Both the agent, and the company. This is something that's really important, for everything to go well. As far as choosing the right agent, work with someone who really communicates well, someone who really works hard for you and lets the buyer and seller know what's going on at all times, both before and after the transaction. To me that's one of the most important factors.

It really tells the story about how easy something is going to go.

Some agents you see operating are not so solid. People have agendas so they operate in that way. Also they don't communicate. There are surprises in the middle of the escrow, which is the worst in this business – when people didn't realize it, or that the buyer wasn't as strong as the seller thought they were. Or problems with the loan that they should have known about and then they get caught at the end, totally surprised. The worst calls I get are the ones at the very end of the escrow period, saying that they can't close or they can't get the loan, or they don't have the money. Those are things that really frustrate the buyer or seller no end.

Also, in multiple offers when buyers lose out on the house they really want, that's when I get the calls. When there is only one house like that in an area for a while and then they have to wait six months or so, the frustration is beyond belief.

A lot of the great brokers of all time, would always say that buyers are very happy when they buy the house. So an agent shouldn't try to be a hero in trying to get the best price always. The buyer wants to live in that house for maybe five, 10, 20 years, and an agent is always a hero when the buyers gets the house they wanted. You're never a hero by losing something and saying, "Well, you know, they wouldn't take our low offer." I just got a call yesterday where the guy said he would've gone up to 5 million. I asked, "Why didn't you tell your agent?" He replied, "The agent said we didn't need to do that."

"Well you lost it."

So the lesson to me is always that everybody feels happy once they've made the deal. If it's the house they want and they really wanted it, they feel happy with it in the end when they get it. So if most agents

The January 2015 Scott Report — 4th Quarter 2014 Summary
Beverly Hills Real Estate Facts, Values, Trends and Opportunities for Homeowners and Buyers

can learn that – to get the deal for their client, of course, within reason of what the client wants to pay.

The same with the seller – just really monitor the seller and monitor the transaction so the seller understands what the good and bad of the transaction is at the time, so that there are no surprises. I know I keep using that word "surprises," but it's the worst thing in this business.

PRICE IS A BIG FACTOR

Price is a big thing. I think that people should really examine the price they're going to put their house on the market for, and examine what they want to do to get the maximum out of it, which they do with the help of a good agent.

The worst thing that is happening now, is as much the seller's fault as it is the agent's. There are some agents that will take a listing if the seller wants $8 million, even though it's only worth $5 million. There are some agents, even though they know the property is worth $5 million that will take it at $8 million, and that's not doing anybody any favors.

Some agents in some companies want to just get inventory no matter what the price is. All that does is create frustration. Again, the seller thinks they really have something, but they really don't.

There are the aberrations. Perhaps 10 - 20% of the things that sell, we never thought would sell at the price. But 80% of the market or 90% most of the time, is really within the realm of what we "comp" it out to be (did a market comparison report on it to determine value).

It is really important to get your property correctly priced. At least for the seller to know what it is. Then, if they want to up it 10% they at least know what it is that it should sell for, and then they know to wait it out a little bit. But the facts are the facts.

The great thing about our computer age is, everything is readily available, so there are no secrets. For both the seller and for the buyer as well. The buyer wants to know how something "comped out" as well.

The bank does too. So it's important. Just because you "sold" it for much more doesn't mean the buyer is going to get a loan. So there are all these things that come into play. Some people who rely on an agent based on a friendship, or a family member, to me, doesn't make any sense. Buy them a cup of coffee, but don't let them list your house.

TRULY SERVING THE CLIENT

The greatest agent is the agent who is truly interested in the client – the ethics and the honesty of going into the marketplace and being truly interested in getting the best result for the client, rather than the other way around, the salespeople who just want to further themselves. It also makes a big difference in their referrals. People will refer people who they had a great experience with, and with whom they felt comfortable. That's what we're all here to do, not only to make the deal right, but also for a referral.

I mean, that's what it's based on, that's how people look at it. If they didn't have a good feeling about the transaction, they will not refer the agent. It's like anything else you do, but here, in real estate, even more so. The numbers are so much larger and fewer. Every agent should look at every client and every transaction not only as a client and a transaction that they're with at the time, but also where it goes from there.

> "It is really important to get your property correctly priced. The facts are the facts."

The January 2015 Scott Report — 4th Quarter 2014 Summary
Beverly Hills Real Estate Facts, Values, Trends and Opportunities for Homeowners and Buyers

This office (Coldwell Banker, Beverly Hills North) is the number one Coldwell Banker office out of approximately 10,000 office nationwide. We have a veteran group of agents and a lot of new people who have added tremendously to the office, plus we have great staff, great assistant managers.

The agents in this office work every area. There are very few offices that can work as many areas as we do. Normally, for instance, if you go to the Brentwood office, you mostly work west of the freeway. If you go to the Sunset Strip office, you're in that area, you can work a little bit out of the area, but you rarely go west of the freeway. In this office, we go west of the 405 Freeway, we go to Malibu, we go to Hancock Park. We go everywhere.

This was started by Jon Douglas. I wish I could say it was me, but it was the Jon Douglas Company. This was their flagship office, so they would hire based on being able to sell everywhere. People loved being in the flagship office because they could go everywhere. We've never just serviced Beverly Hills alone. In fact, when I first came here, Jon Douglas was not a big factor in the flats of Beverly Hills. Now we are a tremendous factor because it's changed. It changes every year.

We've got two or three people to do well in an area. The south office of Coldwell Banker also does very well in a lot of areas. So between us, we do a lot of business, but the competition is quite dramatic now.

Mostly, we have the best agents, and that's really what ends up, hopefully, being the difference in the end, for the clients. We have the best agents, the best backup, and the best global exposure. Most companies say they are global but they really don't compare to what we do. They all say they're international, that's today's buzzword, it's been that way for the last 10 years. But our internet access is to 600 websites. When a client lists with us, their property gets exposure on 600 sites. No one compares to that, but not all consumers are interested in that. Some are only interested in their agent just marketing their house locally.

We have a different style, completely. I know the market; I've lived here my whole life so I know the area. So I bring a little bit of a different philosophy to the office. I'm more hands-on. I'm about, "let's get a great job done for each client."

The good thing about this office is that agents work really hard, and there's a miracle every day. That's what I love, and that's what brings me here. There is always something that makes me say, "Are you kidding me?" So that's the great thing about it, and that's the way agents have a look at it, really.

I keep a framed photograph of that check on the wall. That was from the 80s, back when I was selling. It was from a property on Mulholland Drive. There was one day left on the exclusive for the listing. So I just held a Sunday open house and sure enough Jack Nicholson's lawyer was jogging down the street. He stopped in and said, "You know, we don't want anyone to build here." I said, "Who's we?" He said, "I can't tell you." So I said, "What do you mean?" I wasn't as cynical as maybe sometimes I am now about people just (literally) running into an open house.

He said, "I'm a lawyer, here's my card. I'll meet you at your office later on today." And sure enough he turned out to be a lawyer for Jack Nicholson at Loeb & Loeb. We wrote the offer and made the deal. So I went from one day making nothing to the next day making 100

> "Sure enough, he turned out to be a lawyer for Jack Nicholson at Loeb & Loeb. We wrote the offer and made the deal. This was 1988. Things like that happen every day."

The January 2015 Scott Report — 4th Quarter 2014 Summary
BEVERLY HILLS REAL ESTATE FACTS, VALUES, TRENDS AND OPPORTUNITIES FOR HOMEOWNERS AND BUYERS

thousand. This was 1988. Things like that happen every hour.

This is a fascinating business. It's a people business. When I interview new agents and I ask, What are you in this business for? If they answer, "housing," I say, Go be an architect. Because really it's about people. You've got to evaluate people. For instance, at an open house, you've got to evaluate whom you're going to do business with. You can't physically work with everybody and then simply see if something happens for you.

This is what's so great about this business; that's why people love it. We deal with some of the smartest people in the world.

The January 2015 Scott Report — 4th Quarter 2014 Summary
BEVERLY HILLS REAL ESTATE FACTS, VALUES, TRENDS AND OPPORTUNITIES FOR HOMEOWNERS AND BUYERS

From The Desk of Victoria Scott

An Open Letter to Beverly Hills Homeowners

January 23rd, 2015

Dear Friend,

*Selling or Buying a Home in Beverly Hills Requires
an Agent's Considerable Local Knowledge, Experience
and Professionalism*

There is an art to selling and buying a home in Beverly Hills -- to getting it just right for you, the client. There has to be thorough and current knowledge about the city to ensure you receive important and impartial guidance throughout the process. No transaction should, nor has to, result in anything but optimum value gained. No "unrealized" money should ever be left on the table.

I want to take this opportunity to guide you towards choosing a specialist real estate agent when selling or buying your home in Beverly Hills, and helping you make wise selling or buying decisions especially in this (strong) 2015 market.

Let me explain.

Beverly Hills is a unique real estate market for a number of reasons:

● Only 6800 lots make up the 5.7 square miles of Beverly Hills. This will not increase.

● Beverly Hills is one of the most desired cities in the world -- creative, wealthy, cosmopolitan, cultural and bathed in year-round, gorgeous Californian sunshine -- with its indoor-outdoor lifestyle and appeal.

● The city is fascinatingly diverse in its geography (flats and hills), its proximity to the world's greatest designers, chefs, creative and business minds, its multinational population, its magnificent streets, plus the unmistakable pride of living and working in the city. You feel it in the air, you see it in the streets, you meet it in the stores, coffee shops, cafes and restaurants.

● The City provides constant beautification and maintenance, keeping it meticulously manicured year-round. City services are at-the-ready 24-hours a day (residents, business owners and their employees, streets and neighborhoods are tended to and quickly taken care of).

The January 2015 Scott Report — 4th Quarter 2014 Summary
BEVERLY HILLS REAL ESTATE FACTS, VALUES, TRENDS AND OPPORTUNITIES FOR HOMEOWNERS AND BUYERS

All of this, and more, makes Beverly Hills real estate exclusive and unique. It takes specialist agents and brokers to properly serve and fulfill real estate clients here -- like it does to serve the clients of any specialist market.

Choosing a Beverly Hills Real Estate Professional

Choosing the right real estate professional for your individual and particular sale / purchase makes an enormous, emotional and bottom-line difference to your result.

Here is some impartial advice and guidance worth adhering to:

Working with a real estate professional is not only about how experienced and knowledgeable the agent is – and how specialist she or he is in your particular market – but how much you get along with, and find satisfaction working with, her or him.

It is very much a two-way experience, not just one way. If you do not already know who you would like to work with, I advise that you consider two or three prospective agents before deciding on the one with whom you will work.

Look for these specific attributes and qualities:

1, You – the client – are the most important "ingredient."

You – the client – are the most important "ingredient" of any real estate endeavor. In order to fully understand, appreciate and serve your needs as a client, an agent must first and foremost be interested in you.

Even an agent who is "very good" at selling or buying real estate is not as good – and is unable to achieve as high and satisfying result for the client – as an agent who first and foremost has you and your best interests at heart and also has the knowledge, skill and savvy to deliver them for you.

So look for and choose the agent who's primary business is your business, not "theirs."

2, Look for and choose authority.

The agent who is an authority and adviser rather than "just" a salesperson has more influence, clout and ability not only among peers (which is a substantial "plus" for any seller or buyer), but also with buyers and sellers themselves.

If you are seen to be working with one of the industry's authorities, your property for sale, or your offer on a property, carries more weight. An authoritative and respected professional communicates to the industry and the prospective buyer or seller the quality of your property and your offer. Look for authority and expertise in the agent you choose – which includes the company with whom they are affiliated.

3, Choose the agent most skilled in marketing your property.

With number one and two, choose the agent who is most skilled in marketing your property – ethically yet with punch – to ready-and-qualified-to-buy prospects. Ask them how that will be achieved.

There is a marked difference between simply marketing a property versus marketing specifically to ready-to-buy prospects. Placing one or repeated advertisements, creating a brochure, listing your property on real estate web sites, holding open houses and even creating a video is all good, but is not always sufficient to effectively differentiate your property from "all the rest."

"Differentiation marketing" employs these mediums yet, by effectively differentiating your property from every other – speaking about its particular uniqueness and individuality – it reaches buyers who are ready and qualified to buy a home specifically like yours.

Ask the agent you are considering to talk to you about how your property will be marketed.

Marketing is essential – a professional skill, and an art. Make sure your agent has it. Without skilled marketing you lose out on many ready and qualified prospective buyers who otherwise could have seen and been interested in buying your house.

4, Choose an agent proficient in managing all the variables.

Choose an agent who is proficient in managing the variables of selling or buying.

A highly effective agent is one who is able to choreograph all the variables of representing, marketing, negotiating and ethically guiding the right buyer to a successful escrow a sufficiently and smoothly as possible.

Smooth and skillful management of all the variables involved is critical to every transaction. Each transaction requires coordinating timelines, events and people's expectations. It is management at its finest.

Think of it like planning a wedding – so many details, happenings and emotions are involved, not to mention costs. So you want someone who is nonplussed by normal occurrences. You may not know what "normal" is in a transaction because you may only experience selling or buying a home once every 5 or 10, or 20 or even 50 years! But your agent should – someone who has information or additional support at their fingertips.

Sometimes a remedy is as simple as one phone call. Remember your agent's connections become your connections, and it's good to be well connected.

5, Choose an agent who is not too busy for you.

Choose an agent who has the time to sit down with you and thoroughly listen to your needs and desires, and who is able to spend all the time necessary with you, and for you, throughout – from start to successful finish (and beyond).

Expect your agent to be willing and able to return your phone call, text or email quickly, and as a priority. You should never be unanswered longer than two hours. Most times, there is no reason why you should not expect a response almost immediately. Again, your real estate business should be your agent's priority, and you should feel that it is.

6, Choose an agent who is familiar with your specific neighborhood.

Choose an agent who is conversant in the goings-on outside of your front door -- the benefits and qualities of the area including recent sales activity, cultural activity, and future developments.

Your agent should be able to represent your property within this context. This will substantiate a higher value for your home, both specifically and generally. Higher substantiated value means a greater chance of reaping a higher bottom line profit from a buyer who is well suited for your property.

Even though, as a seller, you are interested in the highest dollar amount for your property, you also gain quiet satisfaction by knowing the new owner will have wonderful enjoyment and gratitude for their new home.

A better suited buyer is a more highly motivated buyer. A motivated buyer is likely to make one or two otherwise difficult concessions during the escrow and still feel excellent about the purchase. This adds so much value to your escrow! An agent who loves the area transfers an educated enthusiasm to the prospective buyer and is typically able to achieve an optimal selling price, and a more confident escrow.

7, Choose an agent who can help you prepare for the sale.

Choose an agent who can help you prepare for the sale even months before your house is ready to be put on the market. It is important that you are able to sit with your agent -- often well before the time you want to sell or buy your house -- to discuss your plans, your preferences and

The January 2015 Scott Report — 4th Quarter 2014 Summary
BEVERLY HILLS REAL ESTATE FACTS, VALUES, TRENDS AND OPPORTUNITIES FOR HOMEOWNERS AND BUYERS

time frames and so on, and to ask questions and receive professional know-how and advice.

Your agent should be able to recommend any needed professionals to help you with readying your house if you decide to make any cosmetic improvements or repairs, and if you do not already have your own people. Also, part of an agent's expertise is knowing how a property should look when it is introduced to prospective buyers – how to show it in its best light.

Although repairs and cosmetic improvements are not necessary (many homes are sold "as-is"), if you choose to freshen up your home in readiness for the sale you will usually see a good, or very good, return on your effort and investment.

Don't be afraid to talk to your agent well before you are ready to sell or buy, even months before. A good agent welcomes this. Early advice can help solidify your decision and direction and help you achieve a far more satisfying and profitable result.

A good agent is always willing to sit down with you and discuss your plans, ideas, your timeline, and talk you through the process of selling or buying. Many people skip this step, but it makes the difference between a smooth experience which speaks to preparedness, versus a last minute rush and on-the-spot decision-making.

Ask yourself, if someone brought you a business proposal which required a substantial financial investment (similar to the value of the home you are either selling or buying), how much time would you want or need before you'd have an answer for that person? Your answer reveals the amount of time you should allow to start preparing for your sale or purchase.

Follow this advice and you will ensure that you not only reap the greatest value from your sale or purchase, but that the whole process runs smoothly, without undue stress, and ends in a successful escrow.

I invite you to call me at **310-849-8880** if you would like me and my team to list and sell your Beverly Hills home -- or to start the conversation. I am at your service.

Warmest regards,

Victoria Scott
CEO, Victoria Scott Estates
Coldwell Banker North Office
301 North Canon Dr, Suite E, Beverly Hills, CA 90210

The January 2015 Scott Report — 4th Quarter 2014 Summary
BEVERLY HILLS REAL ESTATE FACTS, VALUES, TRENDS AND OPPORTUNITIES FOR HOMEOWNERS AND BUYERS

Professional Real Estate Services Provided by Victoria Scott Estates at Coldwell Banker North Office, Beverly Hills, CA 90210

Victoria Scott Estates serves the distinguished Beverly Hills clientele. She and her team provide long-time experience and high-end selling, negotiating and purchasing services specific to Beverly Hills neighborhoods.

Victoria is the daughter of Beverly Hills real estate icon, June Scott. Along with her brothers Peter Whyte and Barry Scott, she continues June's legacy of preeminent service and excellence for every client, family and professional she works with.

Victoria Scott

Her clients include some of Beverly Hills most famous and local business owners, surgeons, GPs, attorneys, entertainment industry producers, developers and builders, international buyers and families.

Victoria gives the full weight of her knowledge and skill to every client and project. She has a refreshing ability that makes the selling and buying process smooth. Her thoroughness and preparedness enables each client to rest assured without undue stress.

Her knowledge and ability to accomplish your goal – combined with her unwavering commitment to every detail and insistence on ethical and transparent practice – makes her one of the most admired real estate professionals in the community.

Call her office at 310-777-6251 to discuss listing your Beverly Hills home for sale, or your interest in purchasing a Beverly Hills residence.

"Through a combination of hard work, professionalism, and an unyielding commitment to meeting your clients' real estate needs, you have managed to keep your performance truly elevated. You have distinguished yourself as a leader and innovator in the real estate profession."

Bruce Zipf
President & CEO, NRT LLC

www.ingramcontent.com/pod-product-compliance
Lightning Source LLC
Chambersburg PA
CBHW041533040426
42446CB00002B/72